BENGAL TIGER AT THE BAGHDAD ZOO

BY RAJIV JOSEPH

DRAMATISTS
PLAY SERVICE
INC.

BENGAL TIGER AT THE BAGHDAD ZOO
Copyright © 2012, Rajiv Joseph

All Rights Reserved

BENGAL TIGER AT THE BAGHDAD ZOO is fully protected under the copyright laws of the United States of America, and of all countries covered by the International Copyright Union (including the Dominion of Canada and the rest of the British Commonwealth), and of all countries covered by the Pan-American Copyright Convention, the Universal Copyright Convention, the Berne Convention, and of all countries with which the United States has reciprocal copyright relations. No part of this publication may be reproduced in any form by any means (electronic, mechanical, photocopying, recording, or otherwise), or stored in any retrieval system in any way (electronic or mechanical) without written permission of the publisher.

The English language stock and amateur stage performance rights in the United States, its territories, possessions and Canada for BENGAL TIGER AT THE BAGHDAD ZOO are controlled exclusively by Dramatists Play Service, 440 Park Avenue South, New York, NY 10016. **No professional or nonprofessional performance of the Play may be given without obtaining in advance the written permission of Dramatists Play Service and paying the requisite fee.**

All other rights, including without limitation motion picture, recitation, lecturing, public reading, radio broadcasting, television, video or sound recording, and the rights of translation into foreign languages are strictly reserved.

Inquiries concerning all other rights should be addressed to the Gersh Agency, 41 Madison Avenue, 29th Floor, New York, NY 10010. Attn: Seth Glewen.

NOTE ON BILLING
Anyone receiving permission to produce BENGAL TIGER AT THE BAGHDAD ZOO is required to give credit to the Author as sole and exclusive Author of the Play on the title page of all programs distributed in connection with performances of the Play and in all instances in which the title of the Play appears, including printed or digital materials for advertising, publicizing or otherwise exploiting the Play and/or a production thereof. The name of the Author must appear on a separate line, in which no other name appears, immediately beneath the title and in size of type equal to 50% of the size of the largest, most prominent letter used for the title of the Play. No person, firm or entity may receive credit larger or more prominent than that accorded the Author. The following acknowledgments must appear on the title page in all programs distributed in connection with performances of the Play:

Original Broadway production produced by
Robyn Goodman, Kevin McCollum, Jeffrey Seller,
Sander Jacobs, Ruth Hendel/Burnt Umber, Scott & Brian Zellinger,
Center Theatre Group, Stephen Kocis/Walt Grossman.

World Premiere produced by
Center Theater Group/Kirk Douglas Theatre
(Michael Ritchie, Artistic Director; Charles Dillingham, Managing Director),
Los Angeles, CA.

Developed at The Lark Play Development Center, New York City.

The following billing must appear on the staff page in all programs distributed in connection with performances of the Play:

Translations/Cultural Consultants: Raida Fahmi and Ammar Ramzi.

For Moisés Kaufman

BENGAL TIGER AT THE BAGHDAD ZOO received its Broadway premiere at the Richard Rodgers Theatre on March 31, 2011. It was directed by Moisés Kaufman; the set design was by Derek McLane; the costume design was by David Zinn; the lighting design was by David Lander; the sound design was by Acme Sound Partners and Cricket S. Myers; the original music was composed by Kathryn Bostic; the production stage manager was Beverly Jenkins; the stage manager was Alex Lyu Volckhausen; and the Iraqi-Arabic translations were by Ammar Ramzi and Raida Fahmi. The cast was as follows:

TIGER	Robin Williams
MUSA	Arian Moayed
TOM	Glenn Davis
KEV	Brad Fleischer
IRAQI WOMAN/LEPER	Necar Zadegan
IRAQI MAN/UDAY	Hrach Titizian
HADIA/IRAQI TEENAGER	Sheila Vand

CHARACTERS

TIGER — Big. Tiger wears clothes. Nothing feline about him.

TOM — American, early 20s, older and wiser than Kev. Unsmiling, tough.

KEV — American, early 20s.

MUSA — Iraqi, 30s.

UDAY — Iraqi, 30s.

IRAQI MAN

IRAQI WOMAN

IRAQI TEENAGER/HADIA — Female.

IRAQI WOMAN — A leper.

PLACE

Baghdad.

TIME

2003.

A note on the Tiger: The Tiger can be any age, although ideally he is older, scrappy, past his prime, yet still tough. He can be any race except Middle-Eastern. His language is loose, casual; his profanity is second nature.

There should be no subtitles for the Arabic.

BENGAL TIGER AT THE BAGHDAD ZOO

ACT ONE

Scene 1

The Baghdad Zoo, night.

Two American soldiers standing guard next to a cage with a Bengal Tiger.

The Tiger stands like a person and faces and speaks to the audience.

TIGER. The lions escaped two days ago. Predictably, they got killed in about two hours. Everybody always gives lions so much credit. But I am bigger than them. I am bigger than those motherfuckers.
TOM. This guy is hungry.
KEV. Sergeant said they fed him.
TIGER. They liked to show off the lions here because they had eight.
TOM. No, he's hungry.
TIGER. Eight fucking lions.
KEV. This place creeps me out. I wanna see some action, not hang around no ghetto-ass zoo with my thumb up my ass.
TIGER. Which is why they had them in that big outdoor lion's den. Which is why they all got away.
TOM. Zoo duty's seen action three nights last week.
KEV. Who's gonna attack a zoo.

TOM. *We're* here. They'll attack *us*. And they've been stealing shit. Like peacocks.

TIGER. All eight of them took off as soon as the wall got blown up.

KEV. I don't know why they wanna kill *us*. We're trying to protect their zoo, you know?

TIGER. Typical lion-like behavior.

TOM. *We* blew the zoo up. Use your head. And these animals are valuable.

TIGER. Three square meals a day, and the idiots take off.

KEV. This guy ain't valuable. So let me see it.

TOM. Again?

KEV. C'mon, Tommy. Let me see it.

TOM. I showed you it already.

KEV. I wanna fire it!

TOM. You're not gonna fire anything.

TIGER. And what happens?

KEV. Come on, man.

TOM. It's not even loaded.

KEV. You told me you always keep it loaded.

TIGER. Ka-boom.

TOM. Well, you're not gonna fire it anyway.

TIGER. I mean, it's the middle of a war. Use your head.

TOM. How many times you gonna want to see it?

KEV. It's bad ass.

TIGER. Leo, the head lion — I mean, they were all named fucking Leo — Leo calls out to me just before he takes off, "Hey, Tiger, you gotta come with!"

KEV. I wrote my brother about it. He said there ain't no such thing as no gold gun. He said guns can't be made outta gold. *(The boys hear a sound.)* What the fuck was that?

TIGER. I said, Leo, you dumb stupid bastard, they're killing anything that *moves*. And Leo — this is right over his head — he yells back, "Suit yourself!" Then he runs off.

TOM. *(Picks up his machine gun.)* Halt! Who goes there!

KEV. *(Yelling, picking up his gun.)* Who's there? We're U.S. Marines!

TOM. Shut up, Kev. *(Shouts.)* Advance and be recognized! *(To Kev.)* Cover me. *(Tom exits.)*

TIGER. *Suit yourself.* I'm still freaking locked up in here, Leo! What're you gonna do, steal the keys and *let me out*? These lions

were dumb as rocks. They think because they can suddenly escape, everyone else can, too. *(Tom enters.)*
TOM. It was that fucking ostrich.
KEV. You shoulda shot it.
TOM. I'm not gonna kill an ostrich.
KEV. Fuck that, man. I don't give a fuck. I'll be like … *(He pretends to shoot his machine gun.)* What's up ostrich, motherfucker? I'll *kill* you, bitch!
TOM. At ease with that shit. This is why everyone thinks you're a fucking idiot, you know that?
KEV. That's what *I'd* do, anyway.
TOM. Sergeant said no more killing animals unless they're a danger.
KEV. Sergeant is a pussy. Can I see it?
TOM. It's in my bag, Kev! Just get it! *(Kev darts to Tom's canvas satchel and pulls out a gold-plated semi-automatic pistol.)*
KEV. Holy shit, man.
TIGER. I won't lie. When I get hungry, I get stupid. I screwed up twelve years back. I just followed the scent, took a bite and then, fhwipp!
KEV. A gold fuckin' gun.
TIGER. This tranquilizer dart comes out of nowhere, and I wake up in Baghdad.
KEV. Sweet ass.
TIGER. So that was depressing.
TOM. You happy now?
KEV. Hell yeah!
TIGER. Imagine, it's your everyday routine … maybe you want to grab a bite, and then whack!
KEV. Yeah, this is the shit right here.
TIGER. Curtains.
KEV. You swear to God this was really Saddam's kid's gun?
TIGER. And you open your eyes and you're in this concrete block.
TOM. Uday.
KEV. Who?
TOM. Uday Hussein.
KEV. Who's that?
TIGER. Tiger of the Tigris.
TOM. Saddam's kid.
KEV. Damn.

TIGER. When you're this far from home, you know you're never getting back.
KEV. This really his gun?
TOM. Yes it was his gun. Who else has a gold-plated gun?
KEV. Damn.
TOM. *(Looking at the Tiger.)* Look at this poor bastard. He's hungry. *(To Tiger.)* You hungry, buddy? *(Tom hits the cage.)* Hey, buddy!
TIGER. Yeah, fuck you too.
TOM. Goddamn! You hear that growl, baby? He's starving.
KEV. How you know for sure? How you know that it was Saddam's kid's gun?
TOM. We raided the mansion. I was there, man. Two-day stand-off.
KEV. Fuuuck …
TIGER. What if my cage *had* gotten hit? What if, ka-boom, there's a big gaping hole in my cage? What do I do then? I'm not gonna go traipsing around the city, like the lions did. No, fuck that.
KEV. What mansion?
TOM. The Hussein brothers' mansion, jackass. Uday and Qusay. They were stacked with gold and shit. Everything in the house was made of gold, practically.
TIGER. But I think I'd step out for a bit. Hang around the zoo. Hunt something. Kill all the people, kill everyone. Eat them.
KEV. What else was gold?
TOM. All their guns. Sergeant got the gold Uzi.
TIGER. Then I'd sleep a little. And then get up, kill some of the animals. Eat them. Sleep some more. But I guess at that point, I'd probably step out. Into the world. Not like the lions did, but still, have to admit, I'm curious.
TOM. The toilet was made of gold.
KEV. No shit. The shitter?
TIGER. The world is probably a fascinating place.
TOM. The *toilet* was gold. Sergeant dismantled the whole thing. I won the seat off him in poker.
KEV. You won a toilet seat?
TOM. *Gold* toilet seat. I won the *gold* toilet seat.
KEV. Where is it.
TOM. Somewhere safe. I buried it.
KEV. Where?
TOM. Yeah, I'm gonna tell you, Kev. I'm gonna tell *you*. Some-

where safe. Between this gun and that toilet seat, I am set. Back home, I'll be sitting pretty.
KEV. Sitting pretty on a gold toilet seat!
TOM. No, dude. I'm not going to *use* it. I'm gonna hit eBay with that shit, you know?
KEV. Man. I haven't seen nothing since I been here.
TIGER. Zoo is hell. Ask any animal. Rather be shot up and eaten than be stuck in a fucking zoo ten thousand miles from where you were supposed to be. Like that polar bear they brought in six years ago. He committed suicide. Some world.
KEV. You got to kill Saddam's kids, man. That's awesome.
TOM. Yeah, it was cool.
TIGER. And the fucking lions! They get it *all*, right? Every captive animal's dream: that a bolt of lightning comes down and ZAP! Frees you in an instant. There it was: freedom! And they blew it. They walked right into the mouth of the beast. Dumb sons of bitches. It's too iffy strutting out into the world like that. I can see them: the eight Leos running through the streets of Baghdad, laughing their heads off. And then — ka-boom — mowed down by artillery. Casualties. A pride of fucking lions.
KEV. I ain't seen shit. Nothing. Not one Iraqi did I get to kill! And I ain't got my dick wet neither! You know back in Vietnam, there was so many Vietnamese bitches all over the place, and everyone got a piece.
TOM. You weren't even born yet.
KEV. I'm just saying. There ain't much pussy in a Muslim country.
TOM. Sergeant got some. Sergeant gets that shit all the time.
KEV. You ever get any Iraqi pussy?
TOM. No, man. Fuck that. I got values. Hand me that Slim Jim. *(Kev hands Tom a Slim Jim, Tom unwraps it and sticks it through the cage, trying to poke Tiger.)* Dumb bastard is so hungry, he don't even know he's hungry.
KEV. Leave him alone. He's barely got any fur left anyhow.
TOM. Eat! Eat it up, man!
TIGER. Don't wanna eat.
TOM. Come on, tough guy. Give me another growl.
TIGER. Leave me alone.
TOM. Atta boy. Get angry. Eat something.
TIGER. *(To audience.)* This is what I'm talking about. Pure stupidity. I'm a fucking Tiger. *(Tom hits Tiger with the Slim Jim.)*

TOM. EAT! *(The Tiger bites Tom's hand off.)* My hand!
TIGER. Yeah your hand! *(Kev shoots the Tiger repeatedly with the gold gun.)*
TOM. Oh God, my hand!
KEV. Tommy! Tommy, you okay? *(Beat.)* I shot him, Tommy! I shot him! *(Tom collapses and passes out. The Tiger, now a ghost, stands outside the cage and can watch as Kev walks over to the cage, pointing the gun at the Tiger's dead body.)* I fucking shot him! I shot him! Oh my God, I shot him!
TIGER. Great. This is just wonderful. I get so stupid when I get hungry! Starts out with a tranquilizer dart. Ends with a bullet.
KEV. He's dead, Tommy! I killed him! *(Beat.)*
TIGER. To die in captivity at the Baghdad Zoo. What a freaking life.
KEV. Who's King of the Jungle *now*, bitch?
TIGER. The lions, you jackass.
KEV. *(Gets on radio.)* Man down! Man attacked by fucking Tiger animal! *(To Tom.)* Tommy, I'm gonna go get help! Stay here! *(Kev exits. The Tiger stares at his own dead body. Beat.)*
TIGER. But I guess I was always going to die here. I guess that was my fate, from the start. But I would have thought maybe I'd have one good day. A day like the Leos had. A brief foray out into the great wide open. And I'm bigger than them. I am bigger than those motherfuckers. *(Beat; he looks at his body.)* So that's what I look like. You go your whole life never knowing how you look. And then there you are. You get hungry, you get stupid, you get shot and die. And you get this quick glimpse at how you look, to those around you, to the world. It's never what you thought. And then it's over. Curtains. Ka-boom.

Scene 2

Musa sits on the floor in an office, writing. There is a laptop at his side and a dictionary.

He writes and then reads what he writes.

MUSA. "Knock knock." "Who's there?" "Operation Iraqi Freedom." "Operation Iraqi Freedom who?" "Operation Iraqi Freedom … bitch." *(Musa stares at the words, shakes his head, frustrated, confused. He flips through the dictionary.)* "Bitch" … "Bitch" … "Operation Iraqi Freedom, bitch." *(He finds the word. Reads it. Frowns and shakes his head and puts the book aside. Kev enters carrying a huge amount of combat gear. He puts it down and catches his breath. Musa stares at him. Kev stares back.)* What is "bitch"?
KEV. What?
MUSA. "Bitch." What is "bitch"?
KEV. Are you calling me a bitch?
MUSA. No. I am asking you what "bitch" means.
KEV. So why you calling me a bitch, bitch?
MUSA. I want to know what it means. "Bitch." The word. I look it up in the dictionary. *(Kev starts donning his gear.)*
KEV. You're the terp.
MUSA. Yes. My name is Musa.
KEV. You going on these night raids?
MUSA. Yes.
KEV. You speak Iraqi?
MUSA. Arabic.
KEV. *Arabic?*
MUSA. Iraqi Arabic.
KEV. So why do you get a computer?
MUSA. This is my own computer. I bought it.
KEV. It have a DVD player?
MUSA. DVD? Yes.
KEV. You got any movies?
MUSA. Movies? Yes. I have a number of movies.

KEV. What movies you got?
MUSA. I have a number of movies. I have *Fast and Furious*.
KEV. You got *Fast and Furious*?
MUSA. Yes.
KEV. I love that movie.
MUSA. It's a good film.
KEV. It's a fucking classic.
MUSA. Yes. *(Beat.)* What is this word "bitch"?
KEV. Why you keep asking me about "bitch"?
MUSA. I know the word. It is derogatory, meaning the female of the dog. But I do not always understand its context. I have looked it up in the dictionary.
KEV. So what's it say in the *dictionary*? Jesus!
MUSA. There are a number of definitions. *(Reads.)* "The female of the dog." "A spiteful or domineering woman." "To complain of or about."
KEV. But it also means, you know, like you're a faggot ass or something.
MUSA. Again, this I don't quite understand.
KEV. You know, like if you're a little pussy or something, or you're being like, you know, a pussy. Then you're being a bitch, you know?
MUSA. No.
KEV. Why do want to know anyway?
MUSA. I speak English, but I don't understand casual American phrases. So when I go with the soldiers, I listen for these phrases and I write them down so that I can better understand the way you speak. It's also why I enjoy watching films.
KEV. You learning English from *Fast and Furious*?
MUSA. I watch *Fast and Furious* because of the cars. I like the cars.
KEV. Yeah, they're sweet ass.
MUSA. But I overheard this the other day. It is a joke. "Knock knock."
KEV. Who's there?
MUSA. Operation Iraqi Freedom.
KEV. Operation Iraqi Freedom who?
MUSA. Operation Iraqi Freedom, *bitch.*
KEV. Dah. That's good.
MUSA. What does "bitch" mean in this instance?
KEV. Well, we got these things called knock-knock jokes, right? And they're —

MUSA. — No, I understand the convention of knock-knock jokes.
KEV. So what's your question? Jesus. I mean, if you're such a smart guy.
MUSA. Never mind. *(Kev finishes putting on his combat gear.)*
KEV. Fuck yeah. Fuck yeah.
MUSA. Why have you dressed in here?
KEV. None of your business, Habib.
MUSA. I mean, this is just office space. Just translators work in here. Why would you dress in here?
KEV. None of your fucking business, I said.
MUSA. Are you new?
KEV. I'm not new.
MUSA. No?
KEV. I've seen action, boy.
MUSA. Me too.
KEV. Yeah, but I have a gun. You, what *you* do, you *talk*.
MUSA. I help you do your job.
KEV. You don't help me with shit, Habib.
MUSA. I see.
KEV. That's why I get this bad ass equipment, see? And that's why you get a fucking laptop. You can boot up and watch *Fast and Furious*, but I live it, bitch. I live *Fast and Furious*.
MUSA. Why am I a bitch?
KEV. Just shut up.
MUSA. What kind of action have you seen?
KEV. What kind?
MUSA. Yes.
KEV. I killed a Tiger.
MUSA. You killed…?
KEV. A Tiger.
MUSA. A Tiger?
KEV. At the zoo.
MUSA. Why?
KEV. He bit off my friend's hand! This Tiger, he attacked him, this guy Tommy, he's like my best friend over here. And so I shot the bastard in the gut. The Tiger, I mean. And he died. I saved Tommy's life, you know? But now he's back in America and everyone's all like … eh … stupid fucking retard, killin' Tigers and shit. Like I did something wrong. I wanted to get the Tiger

and skin him. I wanted to make a carpet out of him, but they wouldn't let me. Can you believe that?

MUSA. Yes, you got gypped.

KEV. That's right! I got fucking gypped!

MUSA. That is one of the casual phrases I have learned. Gypped! *(Kev laughs and smiles at Musa.)*

KEV. Hey. You want to see something?

MUSA. Yes.

KEV. You can't tell anyone you saw this, okay?

MUSA. Okay.

KEV. I'm serious, Habib.

MUSA. Yes. *(Kev looks around covertly. Goes into his bag, pulls out the gold gun. He shows it to Musa.)*

KEV. You see this shit? This was Saddam's kid's gun.

MUSA. What?

KEV. Saddam's kid. I don't know. Last name Hussein. *(Musa stares at the gun. He reaches out for it.)* Uh-uh. No touchy, Habib.

MUSA. May I?

KEV. No touchy.

MUSA. I would just like to … please. May I hold it? *(Kev considers. He likes that Musa wants it.)*

KEV. Okay, but don't get any ideas, Habib. I will waste you. *(Musa takes the gun and stares at it.)* I was at the standoff at the palace, baby. Two-day standoff. We killed those sons of bitches. Both of them. Man, that palace they had? Gold out the ass, man. Gold everywhere. All their weapons were gold! Even their toilet was gold, boy! God damn! *(Musa still stares at the gun, now grasping it in a strange manner. He begins to shake with rage.)* Dude. Habib?

MUSA. You killed them?

KEV. Who?

MUSA. Uday Hussein. Qusay Hussein. You were among the soldiers who killed them?

KEV. Yeah, dude. What? *(Musa shakes, begins to breathe harshly.)* What is *wrong* with you, man? Habib! Relax! *(Musa falls into a crouch, still clutching the gun. Kev tries to grab the gun from him.)* You're going psycho jihadi on me now. Give me the gun! What the fuck? *(Kev struggles to take the gun from Musa and finally does.)* Jesus! What the fuck is your problem? *(Musa sits on the ground motionless, staring at nothing.)* Seriously, Habib. Are you going crazy on me here? Do I need to shoot you?

MUSA. You do not need to shoot me.
KEV. Good, man. 'Cause I don't want to shoot you. What the fuck is your problem, though?
MUSA. I don't have a problem.
KEV. No? Then what was all that shit about? All that shaking around and shit? *(Near tears.)* Jesus! Everything I see, every day. Is just wack, you know? I never see nothing I've seen before. It's just one crazy fucking thing after another. You're a freak, Habib. Freaky-deaky, no shit. *(Kev begins to freak out, shaking, nervous.)*
MUSA. I don't have a problem. Please leave me alone. Please leave me. This room is for translators. Why are you here?
KEV. I got to get dressed!
MUSA. *(Deliberate.)* Go Dress Somewhere Else. *(Beat.)*
KEV. I just need to be alone when I put this stuff on or I don't do it right. It doesn't mean I'm a fucking idiot. I just have to concentrate. *(Beat.)* This is like fifty pounds of gear, man. Kevlar and shit. It's like complicated, you know?
MUSA. Complicated.
KEV. Yeah. Complicated. It's war, you know? Everything is all fucked up. But now I know how to put this shit on. I'm all set. Gonna go out tonight and figure some shit out, right?
MUSA. I suppose so. *(Kev holds out his hand for a high five. Musa just looks at it.)*
KEV. I catch you later, Habib. Come on, man. High five. *(Musa just stares at Kev's hand.)* Come on, man! High five! *(Musa lightly high fives him.)* That's what I'm talking about, bitch. That's what I'm talking about.

Scene 3

In the dark, chaotic sounds of soldiers pounding on the doors of a home. Yelling, screaming, furniture being overturned.

As the sounds continue, lights up on an Iraqi man standing with a sack tied around his head and his hands tied behind his back.

Kev enters with Musa.

A woman runs on and goes to the man. Her sudden entrance goes entirely against procedure and freaks Kev and Musa out.

WOMAN. La-takhthoo! Etle'oo min baitne! Joozoo min edne! *[Don't take him! Get out of our house! Leave us alone!]*

لا تاخذو! اطلعو من بيتتة! جوزو من عدنة!

KEV. Whoa! Get her back!
MUSA. *(To woman.)* Irja-ee. Irja-ee. *[Go back! Go back!]*

ارجعي!

KEV. *(To man.)* I need you down on the ground! Hands behind your — Sir? *SIR?* I need you DOWN on the GROUND! DOWN on the GROUND!
MUSA. *(In Arabic, to man.)* Inteh tehtaj tinzil lil … *[You need go down to —]*

انتة تحتاج تنزل لل...

KEV. Wait, what are you telling him?
MUSA. What?
WOMAN. Makoo shee elkoom ehna! Roohoo! *[There's nothing here for you! Go away!]*

ماكو شي الكم اهنا! روحو!

KEV. What are you telling him?
WOMAN. Me sawaine shee ghalatt. Roohoo! *[We have done nothing wrong. Go away!]*

ما سوينة شي غلط. روحو!

MUSA. I'm telling him what you said!
KEV. What the fuck?
MUSA. I'm *TRANSLATING*!
KEV. *(To man.)* You speak English? Hey, sir, you speak fucking *ENGLISH*?!
MAN. Hathe shee-yreed? [*What does he want?*]

هاذة شيريد؟

WOMAN. Ma a'roof, daykhereboon ilbait. Yreedoon yakhthook wiyahoom! [*I don't know, they're wrecking the house. They want to take you away!*]

ما اعرف، دي خربون البيت. يريدون ياخذوك وياهم!

(Kev pushes the man.)
KEV. You speak fucking English, I said!
MUSA. He doesn't speak English!
KEV. Fuck that, man. Tell him to kneel down. I'm gonna count from five! 5 … 4 … 3 … 2 …
MUSA. *(Over Kev.)* Yireed-kum thnain-nat-koom terka'oon. [*He wants you both to kneel down.*]

يريدكم ثنيناتكم تركعون.

(The man and woman kneel down. Kev bumps into a large wooden chest and nearly falls over.)
KEV. Hey! What's in this chest here? Hey you speaka Englisha?
MUSA. They don't speak English! Stop yelling! You don't need to yell.
KEV. That's what you gotta do, man, or these towelheads will fuck you, man. No offense, but that's like the rules.
MUSA. Just tell me what you want to tell them and I will translate. Okay?
KEV. Don't fucking tell me my business, Habib.
WOMAN. Allahoo akbar, ehne me sawaine shee, bess gooloo shitreedoon? Treedoon takhthoone kulne? Etla'oo! Etla'oo min baitee! [*Oh my God, we've done nothing, but say what do you want? You want to take us all away? Get out! Get out of my home!*]

الله اكبر، احنة ما سوينة شي، بس كولو شتريدون؟ تريدون تاخذونة كلنة؟ اطلعو برة! اطلعو من بيتي!

MAN. Kafee tse-ween masha-kil! Lazim nse-wee lee-reedoo! *[Stop making trouble! We must do what they say!]*

كافي تسوين مشاكل! لازم نسوي ليريدو!

KEV. *(Yelling.)* Shut up! What's in this box?
MUSA. Yireed yu'roof shinoo bil sundoog. *[He wants to know what is in this box.]*

يريد يعرف شنو بلصندوك.

WOMAN. Il sendoog, yreed il sendoog? Yigder yakhooth il sendoog, ukhthe! Bess roohoo, telle'hum koolhum berre! Ehne me sawaine shee ghalatt! *[The box!? He wants the box? He can take it, take it! Just leave, get them all out! We haven't done anything wrong!]*

الصندوك؟ يريد الصندوك؟ يكدر ياخذة، اخذة! بس روحو، طلعهم كلهم برة! ما سوينة شي غلط!

MUSA. She says there are … *(To woman; Arabic.)* Shgil-tee? *[What did you say?]*

شكلتي؟

KEV. Wait what?
WOMAN. Makoo shee hnak! Bess buttaniat, makoo ghair shee! *[There's nothing in there! Blankets and nothing else!]*

ماكو شي هناك! بس بطانيات ماكو غير شي!

MUSA. Nothing! There's nothing —
KEV. That's bullshit. She said a lot more than *nothing*. I don't speak Iraqi, but she said a lot more than *nothing*.
WOMAN. Yireed il sendoog? Gul-le khelee yakhooth il sendoog! Yakhthe we-yrooh! *[He wants a box? Tell him to take the box! Take it and leave!]*

يريد الصندوك؟ كلة خلي ياخذ الصندوك! ياخذة و يروح!

MAN. Sook-tee! Let saw-weeheh engess! *[Be quiet! Don't make it worse!]*

سكتي! لتسويهة انكس!

MUSA. *(To man and woman.)* Raja'en sook-too! Reja'en! *[Please be quiet! Please!]*

رجاء سكتو! رجاء!

KEV. *(Re: the man and woman talking.)* See that's what I'm talking about. *(Kev goes to the man and woman and stands above them in a threatening manner.)* WE ARE HERE TO HELP YOU!
MUSA. You don't need to do this!
KEV. What's in the BOX?!
MUSA. *(To woman.)* Shinoo bil sundoog? *[What is in the box?]*

شنو بلصندوك؟

WOMAN. *BUTTANIAT! BUTTANIAT! [BLANKETS! BLANKETS!]*

بطانيات! بطانيات!

MUSA. *(To Kev; accidentally in Arabic.)* Buttaniat!

بطانيات!

KEV. What? What the fuck did you say!?
MUSA. *(To Kev; in Arabic; frustrated.)* BUTTANIAT! BUTTANIAT!

بطانيات! بطانيات!

KEV. In ENGLISH! Speak English, will you?!
MUSA. What?
WOMAN. Let suy-eh! Gul-le kheli y-buttel y-suy-eh! Joozoo min edne! *[Don't yell! Tell him to stop yelling! Leave us alone!]*

لتصيح! كوله خلي يبطل يصيح! جوزو من عدنة!

KEV. What the fuck!
MAN. Kafee tsuy-heen! *[Stop yelling!]*

كافي تصيحين!

MUSA. Blankets! Sorry! Blankets!
MAN. Makoo ba'ad shee moomkin yakh-thoo! Bess sook-tee! *[There's nothing more for them to take! Just be quiet!]*

ماكو بعد شي ممكن ياخذو! بس سكتي!

KEV. What blankets?!
MUSA. In the box!
KEV. What?
WOMAN. Ukhthoo, boogoo, boogu kulshee edne. Mujremeen, kulkum, kul wahid min edkum. *[Take it, steal it, steal everything we have. Criminals, all of you, every one of you.]*

اخذو، بوكو، بوكو كلشي عدنة. مجرمين، كلكم، كل واحد من عدكم.

MUSA. BLANKETS! In the BOX!
KEV. We'll see about that! We'll fucking see about that! *(Kev walks to the chest and opens it and begins taking out folded blankets. He flaps them open and tosses them randomly.)*
WOMAN.   Hathe shee-yreed? Makoo shee hnak! Hethole buttaniat. *[What does he want? There's nothing there! They're blankets.]*

هاذة شيريد؟ ماكو شي هناك! هذولة بطانيات.

KEV. You see this!? You see?
MUSA. What!? What's wrong?! What's happened?
WOMAN.   Hetholeh bess buttaniat! *[They're just blankets!]*

هذولة بس بطانيات!

(As Kev goes through the blankets, he seems to be more and more desperate, looking for something in the box.)
MUSA. You're supposed to stand guard!
KEV. I'm SUPPOSED TO DO MY JOB! Shut up!
WOMAN.   Hathe shday-sa-wee? Makoo shee il-eh hnak! Hathe mejnoon! Hel-rijal foo-ked akle! *[What is he doing? There's nothing there for him! He's crazy! The man has lost his mind!]*

هاذة شديسوي؟ ماكو شي اله هناك! هاذه مجنون! هل رجال فقد عقله!

(The Tiger enters. Kev sees him, but nobody else.)
KEV. Oh God, no way. *(Kev drops his gun. The woman screams.)*
MUSA. What's happened?! What's wrong?
MAN.   Il khater alle hi shdayseer? Te'alee hna, te'alee yemmee! *[For God's sake what is going on? Come here! Come to me!]*

الخاطر الله هاي شديصير؟ تعالي هنا! تعالي يمي!

MUSA. *(To man and woman.)* Suntteh! Moomkin tsooktoon! *[Quiet! Will you shut up!]*

صنطة! ممكن تسكتون!

WOMAN.   Hathe rah yuktulne! Hathe mejnoon! *[He's going to kill us! He's crazy!]*

هاذة رح يقتلنة! هاذة مجنون!

MAN.   Hi shday-seer? Hi shday-saw-woon? *[What's happening? What's going on?]*

هاي شديصير؟ هاي شديسوون؟

KEV. SHUT UP!
WOMAN. Telle'a minna! Akh ya alla … *[Get him out of here! Oh, God …]*

طلعه منا! آخ يااالله …

KEV. NOBODY MOVE! NOBODY SAY A FUCKING WORD!
MUSA. *(To man and woman.)* Suntteh! *[Quiet!]*

صنطة!

KEV. *(Takes out the gold gun.)* Motherfucker … motherfucker …
MUSA. *(Yelling.)* WHAT ARE YOU DOING!?
KEV. SHUT UP! *(Kev picks up a blanket and throws it.)* You see? What the fuck is that?!
MUSA. That's a blanket.
KEV. What else, huh? What fucking else?!
MUSA. There's nothing there! *(Kev points the gun at Musa. The woman screams.)*
KEV. It's not a fucking blanket! It's him! It's HIM! *(Kev points the gun back at the Tiger.)*
MAN. Te'alee hna, te'alee hna, hethole shday-saw-woon? *[Come over here, come over here, what are they doing?]*

تعالي هنا، تعالي هنا، هذولة شديسوون؟

WOMAN. Ma a'roof, hathe iljundee t-kheb-bell, oo ende museddess … *[I don't know! The soldier is sick in the head, he has his gun …]*

ما اعرف! هاذة الجندي تخبل، و عنده مسدس…

KEV. Everyone needs to shut up.
MUSA. Suntteh! *[Be quiet.]*

اصنطة!

KEV. I can't breathe. I can't breathe. *(Kev starts sporadically removing his gear. Helmet, shirt, eventually his pants come off.)*
WOMAN. Hathe shday-saw-wee? Hathe leysh hee-chee day-saw-wee? *[What is he doing? Why is he doing that?]*

هاذة شديسوي؟ هاذة ليش هيجي ديسوي؟

KEV. *(To Tiger.)* Bring it, Tiger. I'm right here, ready, bitch. Don't need no Kevlar, no flak, fuckin-A, just me and you. Me and you Tiger, I'm ready. I'M READY! *(He starts to cry.)* I did it once, I can do it again … I can kill him again …

MUSA. No. No killing. The gun. Give it to me. It's me.
KEV. I didn't want to do it.
MUSA. I know. Here. Give it to me … Yes. Yes. Yes. *(Musa slowly takes the gun from Kev. Kev starts sobbing and collapses. The woman gets up and starts screaming at him, throwing the discarded blankets at him.)*
WOMAN. Ente la shai', ente ma i'ndek shee, inte mejnoon, farigh, kulkum, Demetrio haeyatne b gheba'kum oo lu'abkum il ashwa'i-yeh! *[Nothing, you've got nothing, you're crazy, empty, soulless fool, all of you, ruining our lives with your stupid, mindless game!]*

انت لا شيء، كلشي ما عندك، انت مجنون، فارغ، ما عندك رحمة، كلكم،دمرتو حياتنة بغبائكم و لعبكم العشوائية!

KEV. I'm sorry! I'm sorry! I'm sorry!
WOMAN. Ente! Wean rayih? *[You! Where are you going?]*

انت! وين رايح؟

MUSA. Ani rah-arooh. *[I'm leaving.]*

اني رح اروح.

(Musa looks at the gold gun and then puts on his pants and starts to leave.)
WOMAN. Ente det-boog, mithilhum, haramee, haramee a'adee! *[You're stealing, just like them! Stealing, a common thief!]*

انتة دتبوك، عينا مثلهم! حرامي، حرامي عادي!

MUSA. Joozee minnee. *[Leave me alone.]*

جوزي مني.

WOMAN. Rooh, rooh ilbaitek ya kha'in, ya haramee! *[Go! Go home, you traitor, you thief!]*

روح! روح البيتك يا خائن، يا حرامي!

MUSA. Hathe moo melteh! … *[This gun, this gun does not belong to him.]*

MAN. Met gooleelee hi shdayseer! Tigdereen tbettileen syah, il khattir alle? *[Would you tell me what's happening! Will you stop shouting, for God's sake?]*

م تكوليلي هاي شديصير! تكدرين تبطلين صياح، ال خاطر الله؟

(The woman looks at Kev, now half-buried under blankets.)
WOMAN. *(Quietly to her husband.)* Hoo-eh al ga'. Te'al. Te'al ... *[He's on the ground. He's crazy. He's sick. Come ... come, we'll leave ...]*

هوة عل كع. هاذة مجنون. هاذة مريض. تعال تعال، خلي نروح...

(Woman and man begin to exit; to Kev.) Rooh el-je-hen-nem! *[Go to hell! Leave us alone and go to hell!]*

روح الجهنم! جوز من عدنة و روح الجهنم!

KEV. I'm sorry ... I'm sorry ... I'm just gonna stand here ... I'm just gonna stand here standing guard. Sir, yes sir ... Sir, yes ... sir ... I'M SORRY! Man down! Man down! Man attacked by ... Man attacked by ... Man attacked. I shot him, Tommy. I shot him. I fucking shot him. He's dead, Tommy, I killed him. I'm okay ... I'm okay ... I'M okay! *(The woman and man exit. Kev huddles in the corner. Lights illuminate a garden in Baghdad. The garden is filled with large topiary animals carved out of hedges, but they are ruined, burned and skeletal. Bombs go off in the distance. The Tiger examines the topiary.)*

Scene 4

Tiger wanders the garden of topiary. The bombs in the distance cease. He looks around at the garden.

TIGER. It would have been better to have died young. I'm an old ghost! There's a gang of teenage rhesus monkeys down at the zoo who got blown up by an IED, and they're carrying on like a bunch of morons, milking the afterlife for all its worth. You want my advice? Die young, die with your friends. It's the way to go. *(Referring to topiary.)* I mean, what the fuck is this supposed to be? Animals made out of plants? Vegetative beasts? I've been walking around this city for days now, taking it all in, and nothing was very much of a surprise until I wandered into this garden here. I mean ... Who *does* this? *People.* First they throw all the animals in a zoo, and then they carve up the bushes to make it look like we never left.

Insult to injury. Insult to injury. *(Bombs go off in the distance. The Tiger cringes behind a hedge. The bombs cease.)* I don't know why I'm so scared. You figure getting killed might be the last bad thing that can happen. The worst thing. I'll tell you right now: It's not the worst thing. See, all my life, I've been plagued, as most Tigers are, by this existential quandary: *Why am I here?* But now ... I'm dead, I'm a ghost ... and it's: *Why aren't I gone?* I figured everything just ended. I figured the Leos ... just ended. The suicidal polar bear ... bones and dust. It's alarming, this *life* after death. The fact is, Tigers are atheists. All of us. Unabashed. Heaven and hell? Those are just metaphorical constructs that represent "hungry" and "not hungry." Which is to say, why am I still kicking around? Why me? Why here? It doesn't seem fair. A dead cat consigned to this burning city doesn't seem just. But here I am. Dante in Hades. A Bengal Tiger in Baghdad. *(Beat.)* You didn't think I knew Dante, did you? Now that I'm dead, I'm having all sorts of revelations about the world and existence. Things just appear to me. Knowledge, the stuff of the universe, it just sort of floats into me ... Or maybe I'm floating into *it*. But it doesn't help. No matter how much I learn, I'm still trapped. I just thought I'd be gone by now. Why aren't I gone? Will someone please tell me why I'm not gone from here!? *(Far off in the distance, the Muslim call to prayer is heard. The Tiger listens to it.)* You hear that? That call to prayer? A constellation of minarets surrounds this garden, each one singing in a different key. They come in like a fog, five times a day. Different mosques, all over the city, calling out to God, voices intermingling in the air. *(Beat.)* When an atheist suddenly finds himself walking around after death, he has got some serious re-evaluating to do. *(The call to prayer continues.)* Listen! Calling out to God in this mess. *God.* Can you believe it? *(A loud bomb goes off and the Tiger instinctively covers himself with his arms, and then looks skyward.)*

Scene 5

Kev lies on a hospital bed.

Tom enters.

KEV. Tommy?
TOM. Hey. What's up.
KEV. You're back.
TOM. I came back. Check it out. Bionic hand.
KEV. Holy shit.
TOM. They do you up right. I'm like RoboCop.
KEV. Why'd you come back?
TOM. Didn't want to go out like that. Besides, I had stuff I needed to get.
KEV. Like your toilet seat?
TOM. Yeah, that's one thing. And my gun.
KEV. Let me see your hand.
TOM. Check it out.
KEV. That's bad ass.
TOM. Yeah.
KEV. They've had me in here like a week now.
TOM. What happened?
KEV. It was fucked up.
TOM. Yeah?
KEV. We were doing these night raids? And I went around the back and booked it upstairs? I go in this room, this motherfucker comes out from under the bed. Clocked me in the face. I was out. Next thing I know, I'm on my way here. I wanna get back, you know? This is bullshit. But they keep running tests. They keep telling me they're running tests.
TOM. Yeah.
KEV. How was America.
TOM. It was all right.
KEV. You get any Mickey D's?
TOM. Yeah, I got some. Right before I came back.

KEV. What'd you get?
TOM. What did I order?
KEV. Yeah, at Mickey D's.
TOM. I don't know. Big Mac.
KEV. Big Mac combo?
TOM. Yeah. With the fries and coke.
KEV. I always get McChicken combo.
TOM. Yeah, that's good, too.
KEV. What else you do there.
TOM. I don't know. Got this.
KEV. You get your dick wet?
TOM. No, man.
KEV. You didn't? All the way back to the States and you didn't? You even see any bitches back there?
TOM. Yeah, sure. At the hospital. My nurse.
KEV. You tap that?
TOM. No, man.
KEV. You didn't tap that?
TOM. No, man, Jesus. I got surgery for my hand, okay? I wasn't thinking about getting laid.
KEV. I wish I could get some pussy.
TOM. Yeah. Sure. *(Long pause.)*
KEV. You know that Tiger?
TOM. Yeah.
KEV. I shot him with your gold gun.
TOM. Yeah, I know. I was there. Remember?
KEV. I'm just saying.
TOM. You have it?
KEV. What?
TOM. The gold gun, do you have it?
KEV. Not with me.
TOM. Not with you?
KEV. I told you, man. I'm out on a fucking night raid, next thing I know I'm on my way here. It's not like I had time to pack, you know what I'm saying?
TOM. Where's the gun?
KEV. Somewhere safe.
TOM. Where?
KEV. I don't know man, where's your toilet seat?
TOM. None of your business, Kev. Where's my gold gun?

KEV. You know what, man? I saved you. Okay? I saved your life.
TOM. I don't care what you did, where's my gun?
KEV. It's in your momma's ass.
TOM. What?
KEV. I said: Your gun? It's shoved up your mother's ass. She put it there herself.
TOM. Kev. Do you know that my mother is dead?
KEV. She is?
TOM. Yeah.
KEV. Aw shit, man, I'm sorry, I didn't mean to go off on the moms. I was just saying, you know? I thought you came to visit me and see how I was doing and catch up and everything.
TOM. The gun is mine. I want it back.
KEV. You got your toilet seat! That's gotta be worth way more.
TOM. We're not gonna argue about this.
KEV. You should just give it to me. Be a decent fucking guy, you know? I killed a Tiger with it. *(Tom sticks his prosthetic hand in Kev's face.)*
TOM. Look at this. Look at this, motherfucker!
KEV. What? God, what's your problem?
TOM. I lost my hand! It's gone, do you get that, asshole?
KEV. Yeah, I know, I can see! I was there!
TOM. I was gonna go home and work for my uncle. What am I supposed to do now? I lost my right hand!
KEV. Dude, that thing is top of the line. You're like RoboCop.
TOM. No I'm not. I'm a stupid handicapped jerk. I didn't even get a Purple Heart.
KEV. That sucks.
TOM. Yeah, that sucks. So I got some gold that I can get and so maybe I have a fucking livelihood when I get back.
KEV. A livelihood?
TOM. Yeah, that's like what the meaning of your life is.
KEV. So what, your livelihood's gonna be having a gold toilet seat and a gold gun?
TOM. No ...
KEV. 'Cause that sounds like kind of a wack-ass livelihood, you know?
TOM. Just shut the fuck up about it.
KEV. Tommy, you ever think about him?
TOM. Who?

KEV. The Tiger.
TOM. He *bit off my hand.*
KEV. You ever see him?
TOM. What?
KEV. You ever see the Tiger? Like just hanging around?
TOM. ... The Tiger.
KEV. Yeah. Or talking.
TOM. What are you talking about?
KEV. I'm asking you a question!
TOM. Yeah, what? What is your question?
KEV. I'm asking you!
TOM. What?!
KEV. I'm asking you, you ever see that Tiger around or anything?
TOM. The Tiger is dead. *(The Tiger enters, sees them, but hangs back.)*
KEV. I know the Tiger is dead, I killed the fucking Tiger, I'm asking you if you ever seen him. Like his ghost.
TOM. No, Kev. I've never seen the Tiger's *ghost*. I don't believe in ghosts. Especially I don't believe in animal ghosts.
KEV. I got to tell you something, man.
TOM. Jesus.
KEV. Seriously, man, can I tell you something? You're like the only person I can tell this stuff to.
TOM. I don't even really *know* you, man.
KEV. Can I just tell you something? Please?
TOM. Fine.
KEV. I mean, I'm trying to tell you something!
TOM. I said fine! Okay!
KEV. Trying to be like a normal guy, you know? Trying to tell you something. Something wack. Something kind of wack, okay?
TOM. Would you just tell me?
KEV. Okay. *(Beat.)* So look. You know I said I was on that night raid?
TOM. Yeah. And the dude came out from under the bed and whacked you upside the head. I know.
KEV. Okay, so I'm like lying there, right? And the dude takes off, right? So I'm alone in the bedroom.
TOM. You're alone in the bedroom.
KEV. And the ghost of that Tiger walked into the room ...
TOM. The ghost of the Tiger ...
KEV. I'm telling you, man, it was crazy. But he wasn't like how he was in real life. He was, like, walking on his hind legs.

TOM. No shit. His hind legs.
KEV. Yeah, and he could talk!
TOM. He could talk, what did he say?
KEV. He started babbling all this bullshit to me, and then I fainted.
TOM. You fainted?
KEV. Yeah, man, I mean, I was freaking out.
TOM. And then what?
KEV. That's the thing. I don't remember much after that.
TOM. That's a pretty stupid fucking story.
KEV. You're not listening to me!
TOM. What?
KEV. I didn't finish yet!
TOM. Well then finish! *(Kev gathers himself.)*
KEV. … Trying to tell a story here …
TOM. Tell the story or I'm leaving.
KEV. Forget it.
TOM. Forget it. Jesus, you are retarded, you know that? Where's the gun, Kev?
KEV. I thought you came to see me.
TOM. Well, I didn't come to see you, Kev. What am I, your mother?
KEV. Dude, my mom is dead.
TOM. No she's not.
KEV. So?
TOM. Oh my God! You have got to be the dumbest piece of shit in the entire fucking world.
KEV. Whatever, man! Did you even get the letter I sent you? *(Beat.)*
TOM. Yeah. I got the letter.
KEV. I wrote you a fucking letter, dude.
TOM. I know, I … Thanks. Thanks for the letter you sent me.
KEV. You got it?
TOM. Yeah. I got it right after my first surgery.
KEV. Yeah, I'm good at writing letters and shit.
TOM. I didn't ask you to write me.
KEV. I know you didn't. I ain't no faggot.
TOM. I didn't say you were.
KEV. I wrote you a letter, man! I mean, I saw what happened to you. Do you even remember? Do you even remember that Tiger biting your hand off?
TOM. I remember enough.

KEV. Well, fuckin'-A! I don't exactly think that's, like, normal. Even for war and shit. I was glad to kill that Tiger. I was glad I got to save your life, Tommy. That's what people do when they have a friend and shit.

TOM. Well, thanks.

KEV. Don't mention it. We're partners, you know? We been through battle together, Tommy.

TOM. Do you know where you *are*, Kev?

KEV. The *war*, man.

TOM. No, I mean here.

KEV. Hospital.

TOM. They think you're crazy.

KEV. I ain't crazy.

TOM. You weren't attacked by no Iraqi from under the bed, either.

KEV. You weren't even there.

TOM. You're going nuts.

KEV. No man, I'm cool.

TOM. Gulf War Syndrome, you little bitch.

KEV. I do not!

TOM. You are fucked, man.

KEV. You don't really have a great bedside manner, you know what I'm saying, Tommy?

TOM. They got you on suicide watch.

KEV. That's not true.

TOM. Yeah, they do.

KEV. Bullshit, man! If they did, they wouldn't be leaving sharp objects and shit around, you know? They wouldn't leave sharp objects around my bed for me to find!

TOM. What are you talking about?

KEV. I'm talking about the Tiger!

TOM. The Tiger is DEAD!

KEV. He's not, Tommy. He's right here.

TOM. Where.

KEV. Here. In this room. He hangs out here all the time. He's here right now, Tommy. *(Tom starts to leave. Starts to cry.)* Tommy. Don't leave. You're my best friend.

TOM. I am not your friend.

KEV. Yes, you are. You are, man. And I need you, okay? I'm so scared. He's everywhere, you know? Everywhere I look is that stupid fucking Tiger.

TOM. Well, that's your psycho problem, Kev. Not mine. Now, I have some gold left that I have to get before I leave here, and if I don't get the gun back from you, I'm gonna kill you. Understand? *(Tom exits.)*
KEV. Aw shit, man.
TIGER. Nice guy.
KEV. Shut up.
TIGER. I just remembered something: Sixteen years ago I killed two children. A little girl and a little boy. Sister and brother.
KEV. Fucking dead-ass ghost motherfucker. Just hanging around, trying to make everyone think I'm some crazy-ass piece-of-shit grunt.
TIGER. This was back in the Sunderbans, in West Bengal. Home! The only place these crazy stripes actually camouflage me.
KEV. I'm sorry! Okay? I'm sorry I shot you!
TIGER. I'm telling you, for the most part, I'm very shy! I like to sit back and wait for something to walk by so I can kill it and eat it. I'm a simple guy with simple tastes.
KEV. I wrote my brother about you. He said you're just a figment of my imagination and shit. He said you were just one of those fucked up things about being in war. So what's up now? You don't even exist, bitch! Except for me! Except for me.
TIGER. Anyhow, the two children had strayed away from their village. The girl was collecting wood or something. I watched them curve around a corner. I was absolutely still. The little boy, at one point, turned and looked directly at me, into my eyes. But he didn't register the significance. He never did.
KEV. You know what though? Fuck Tommy. My brother is a hundred times better than Tommy. If I was on suicide watch, then they wouldn't've left shit behind that I could ... you know, shit like this? *(Kev lifts his mattress up and takes out large, sharp piece of metal, like an old knife or scrap metal.)* Shit like this!
TIGER. I was hungry. They were food.
KEV. If you don't get the fuck out of my head, bitch, I will kill us both. Don't think I won't do it. I killed you once, I'll kill you again!
TIGER. And I caused untold misery to the parents of those children. But what could I do? I'm a Tiger.
KEV. Get Out Of My Head!
TIGER. It wasn't cruel. It was lunch! A basic primordial impulse isn't cruel! But what if it *is*? What if my every meal has been an act

of cruelty? What if my very nature is in direct conflict with the moral code of the universe? That would make me a fairly damned individual. After all, *lunch* usually consists of the weak, the small, the stupid, the crippled. Because they're easier to kill.

KEV. You want my hand? You want to eat my hand, just like you did Tommy? Maybe then you'll leave me alone, just like you left Tommy alone! *(Kev starts cutting his wrist. Trying not so much to slit his wrists, as to actually cut his hand off.)*

TIGER. I'm guilty! That's why I'm stuck here. I'm being punished. But you'd think the twelve years in a zoo, caged, never hunting, never killing, never breaking God's ridiculous LAW ... you'd think I would have atoned for my Tigerness. But maybe that's my way out of here. Assuming God exists, and assuming this punishment has a reason, I have to atone. I need you tell me: How do I do it?

KEV. Eat it, take it. Eat my fucking hand, I don't want it!

TIGER. I don't want your hand. I want your help.

KEV. I'll get a new one like Tommy. Fucking RoboCop and everything. See? I can still do what I want. I can do whatever ... whatever I want, and no faggot ass Tiger is gonna ... is gonna ... Yeah. *(Kev dies and crumples in a heap on the bed. Tiger goes to Kev, looks him over.)*

TIGER. *(Realizing.)* Shit. I bite off the one kid's hand. And then I drive this one to suicide. *(Tiger shakes his head. To audience.)* I am digging myself into one hell of a fucking hole. *(Tiger exits.)*

Scene 6

Musa sits at a table in his home. He looks exhausted and depressed. He holds the gold gun and stares at it.

The front door opens. Uday Hussein enters carrying the severed head of his brother, Qusay.

Uday is joyously psychotic. He is delighted by just about everything. However, he should never laugh maniacally.

UDAY. Knock! Knock! *(Musa looks up, but does not respond.)* I said: Knock! Knock! You are to answer "Who Is There?" *(Beat. Uday speaks sometimes to the head of his brother, sometimes to Musa.)* He's no fun today! You're no fun today! *(Beat.)* Fine, I will say! "Who Is There?" "Knock knock!" "Who is there?" "Uday and Qusay!" "Uday and Qusay WHO?" *(Uday walks up to the table where Musa sits, puts his hands on the table and bends down so he is nose to nose with Musa.)* Uday and Qusay HUSSEIN, motherfucker! *(Beat.)* Look, Qusay! It is Mansour. My trusted gardener. But he is not keeping the land any longer. He has a gun! Qusay, he has a gun! *(Uday looks at the gun more carefully.)* Well, what is *this*? Qusay! This is *my* gun! It is my gold-plated semi-automatic pistol. Crafted in Riyadh! Qusay, isn't that remarkable? *(Uday puts Qusay's face to his ear, as if Qusay were whispering to him.)* Qusay says you are a cockroach piece of mothershit worth zero weight in gold. Qusay, his English is not as good as my own. But I like this, I like this *piece of mothershit*, because that is what you are, you piece of mothershit peasant. *(Musa points the gun in Uday's face.)* It is not polite, when you have guests, to shove a gun in their face. I imagine you know this, and so the sting is all the worse. I do not like rudeness.
MUSA. Allahu akbar.
UDAY. *(With fury.)* SHUT UP! *(Uday walks around the table, behind Musa, and sticks the gun to the back of Musa's head.)* How does this feel? How does it feel to have this beautiful weapon pressed against your worthless skull? Qusay! Should I shoot this peasant? *(Qusay*

nods. loud, joyous, about to shoot.) Fine! Thank you for claiming my gun! Thank you! Thank you! Thank you!
MUSA. *(Arabic.)* La' reja'en! Le tuktulnee! Reja'en le tuktulnee! Reja'en! *[No, please! Don't kill me! Please don't kill me! Please!]*

لاء رجاء! لا تكتلني! رجاء لا تكتلني! رجاء!

UDAY. *(Takes the gun away from Musa's head. Cheerful.)* Okay okay okay okay okay. *(Uday walks around, suddenly in a very reflective mood.)* I went looking for my brother after they killed me. All I found was his head. How do you like that? Poor Qusay. I wonder if he's walking around with my head. That would be funny. I find all this very funny, Mansour. Funny, funny, funny. *(Uday pulls up a chair and sits at the table, across from Musa. Truly aggrieved.)* But people don't like me. They say I am a bad man. Evil. A torturer. They say I tortured people. *(Beat.)* Of course I fucking tortured people. When you have people who have wronged you, who have attempted to kill you or your father or your brother, or you have people who look lasciviously upon your sisters and your wife and your girlfriend, and these men have felt it in their hearts that they would kill you and would wipe everything that has become you off the face of the earth, let me tell you, my friend, you would torture them. *(Uday speaks with great relish, as if it were a great joke, or as if describing a delicious and wonderful recipe.)* You would … tie them up … and you would beat the soles of their feet with wet bamboo until they couldn't walk. And then you'd laugh and break their ribs. And you'd pull out their teeth and their toenails and then watch them try to run away again. This is better than any movie you've ever seen! And then once they have tired of this, and they have given themselves up to you, ready for death, then you deny them this death and you bring in THEIR women. And you have your way with them. Because to watch your wife get fucked by a man who is about to kill you, well, that is a piece-of-shit day you are having, my friend. *And that is why you don't ever fuck with Uday Hussein! (Uday leans forward, looking at Musa intently.)* Knock knock! Anyone home? I just told a funny joke, and you don't laugh, and you don't speak to me, and you are very rude, Mansour. Very rude. *(Uday kicks back again, soliloquizing.)* But yeah, man, I am dead. I get about 26 bullets from here to here on me. The Americans got me. Me and Qusay. And then what do they do? These U.S. fucking troops? What do they do? They come into my home and they steal

everything I have, like common little thieves. Like piranhas. I *had* piranhas, I would know. And it is these hungry, greedy little Americans, who you work for. You work for them to kill us. To steal our oil. To fuck us in the ass, Mansour.
MUSA. No.
UDAY. *No?*
MUSA. I do not work for the Americans.
UDAY. You can lie to me, Mansour, but you cannot expect me to lap up your shit like the dogs you work for. *You*, Mansour: a traitor in everyone's midst.
MUSA. I am a different person now.
UDAY. No, piece of mothershit. You are the same. And you lie, Mansour. You lie to me.
MUSA. I do not lie.
UDAY. You lie! Why do you lie to me?! You are thinking you can slip one past me? Who am I?
MUSA. You are dead.
UDAY. Good! Yes! I am dead! And yet, here I am … roaming around Baghdad. Uday Hussein will not go away, Mansour. He is not so simply shot down by a bunch of teenage Ronald McDonalds who think they are the hot shit of 2003. Americans! Always thinking that when things die, they go away. *(Uday offers a cigar to Musa.)* Smoke?
MUSA. No, thank you.
UDAY. It's a Cuban! *(Re: the good cigar.)* Cubans. Fuck me, man. Fuck me in the ass. Breathe it in. Even a dead man loves a Cuban. *(Beat.)* I'm doing good things here, Mansour. My pure existence causes destruction. Everything going down in the streets? The war still being fought? What they call the insurrection? I am the insurrection, Mansour. It is me! *(Beat.)* You're not impressed? Oh, what's wrong, Mansour? Are you still mad about that little thing with your sister? *(Musa doesn't answer.)* I bet you are. I bet you are angry with Uday. But you worked for me, and so I have rights, and so shut up. *(Musa, breathing heavily, suddenly screams, jumps to his feet, kicking the table, and finally collapses on the floor.)* Okay, good. Yeah, crybaby. You can go and cry like a baby.
MUSA. What do you want.
UDAY. But that is not the question, Mansour. The question is what do *you* want? You find yourself in a fucked-up situation all of a sudden, my friend. *(Uday holds the gold gun out in front of*

them.) This gun was a gift to me from a Saudi sheikh. I can't even remember his name. They're all faggots, the Saudis. You know? He gave me this thing and, man, it was the best thing I ever got in my life. That's when I started having everything turned into gold. All my guns, kitchenware, tools, my bedposts, my toothbrush, even the toilet, sahib. Shitting on gold, man! That is the king's way, I am telling you!
MUSA. *(Quietly.)* King Midas.
UDAY. What?
MUSA. *(Quietly.)* Nothing.
UDAY. What did you say? *(Beat.)* You said "King Midas," is that what you said? *(Beat.)* And then you say, never mind, because me, Uday Hussein doesn't know who King Midas is? *(Uday grabs Musa by the hair, pulling his head back.)* The Midas touch! You think I am like Midas? No no, my man, I am better than him, because I don't need magical powers, because I don't need them. And then if I had them, how would I be able to do this? *(Uday grabs Musa by the hair and slams his face into the desk. Musa falls to the ground.)* And this! *(Uday kicks Musa in the stomach and then spits on him.)* You think I want to transform shit like you into gold? Is that what you think, Mansour?
MUSA. … No …
UDAY. No! Absolutely right. No. *(Uday picks up the gold gun.)* You take this back, Mansour. And you know those stupid kid Americans who stole it, they are criminals, just like everyone else. They want it back, but now you have it. So you know what you have now? You have some leverage!
MUSA. I won't do anything for you.
UDAY. Oh, but it's not *for me*, Mansour. I'm here, but I don't need anything. I have you. I have Qusay's head, I have Iraq, just as I always have. And I'm never going to go away. Look at me. What are you going to do with your life? Where are you going to get work as a gardener? There's nothing left to garden, my man. And you think the Americans are going to employ you forever? They're already retreating. And they're going to leave you here with nothing green and nothing to work with except a big pile of shit. All you have is me and my gun. *(Uday gives the gun to Musa. Musa takes it. Uday grabs Qusay's head and listens, as if Qusay is whispering to him. Uday laughs at Qusay's wit.)* Qusay is funny. He remembers your sister, too. Hadia. Haadeeeaaahhh. Do you know what the thing

about your sister was that we loved? *(Musa drops his head in defeat.)* Mansour. Look at me. Do you know what was interesting about her? The way she quivered, Mansour. She was like one of those sculptures you were doing in my garden. What did you call those animals you made? What is that called, Mansour? You tell me, but I am always forgetting.
MUSA. Topiary.
UDAY. Topiary! I love this topiary! You are the real artist, you know that, Mansour? *(Seeing Musa's grief.)* What? What do you want, you brought her to my garden! You brought your little virgin sister to ME! I take what is mine, boss. I take it. And you should have heard her. Such a little creature make such a great noise. What a mess that was, my man. Maybe someday you can make a topiary out of your sister. You can carve her out of the hedges. And she can quiver in the wind. You need to start working again, Mansour. All your animals have died. *(Uday exits, leaving Musa with the gun.)*

End of Act One

ACT TWO

Scene 7

The Tiger appears.

TIGER. This place is lousy with ghosts. And the new ones are irritating. They're walking around, wide-eyed ... *What happened to me? Where am I?* You're dead and you're in Baghdad. Shut up. Anyhow, the other day, I'm walking down the street. The street is literally ON FIRE. And I see this little girl. Her life is like a soap bubble, and then pop! She's here, in the middle of the street, looking up at me. And she says to me: What are you? And I tell her, I'm a Tiger. She asks me am I going to eat her. And I say, no, I gave up eating children. She says why? And I say, I don't know, it's this philosophy I'm working out about sin and redemption since God is apparantly nuts. And the girl just kind of looks at me. And I'm like: Think about it, if God's watching, why'd he snuff you out? Why are you standing here, alone, in a burning street, with a dead Tiger? Why is half your face gone? And she says, yeah, but why'd you give up eating children? And I tell her the bit about the two kids in the forest, and how I keep thinking about them and how I have all this guilt. She doesn't understand that. The guilt thing. She doesn't have any guilt. And I'm like, of course you don't. What did you ever do? Nothing. She tells me she's afraid. I tell her I am too. Which you'd think would be comforting, given the circumstances, but somehow, being blown to bits and then coming face to face with the likes of *me* ... Well, the girl starts to cry, you know? Her one eye, cries. And I say, don't cry. But she cries harder. And so I say to her: Hey, do you want to see something? And she stops crying for a second. And she's like, what? And I say it's a ... I tell her it's a garden. And she looks at me as if to say, big fucking deal, like I haven't seen a garden before? And I say, no, it's a special garden. And I don't know why I say this, but I say, it's God's garden. I tell her it's God's garden. He likes gardens, see. He tests us in them, he tempts us in them, he builds them up and tears them apart. It's like his fucking hobby. And she's skeptical, I can see that, but I bring her here and she sees these plants, these animals, and she's never seen anything like them. And I nailed it, because she's not crying anymore. She's walking around the garden, pointing. *A camel! An elephant! A lion!* Fucking kids, you know? And I mean, this whole time, I'm talking out of my ass, this business about God's garden, etcetera. Maybe she knows I'm bullshitting, too. The girl is no dummy, even if she does only have half a brain. But for a second we both look up at these ruined shrubs and think, okay, Man: You work in Mysterious Ways. We get it. And I feel this swell of hope. And then she turns to me and she's like: *When will He get here?* What? She says, *When will God get here? If this is his garden, then he has to come to it, he has to tend to it. Look! The green is all burned. This animal has lost his head.* Well?! What am I supposed to tell her? I'm asking You to tell me. Because if You don't, I'm going to have to watch her cry again. I'm gonna have to sit here and watch that little single eye of hers well up with tears … And her brain will fill up, as mine did, and she'll understand the Universe. And then her spirit or body or whatever You've left us with, it will go on to other things. And this moment, *this fucking moment* when she appraises a ruined piece of beauty with her one good eye, *this moment* will become extinct. Just like fucking You. Is that what You WANT? *Say Something!* THIS ANIMAL HAS LOST HER HEAD! Speak through me, or through her, or through someone, but speak, *God*, speak!

Scene 8

A back room in a converted officers building. Tom sits at a chair. Across the room a teenage Iraqi girl sits. She wears a hejab headscarf, but a tight T-shirt and blue jeans. They don't look at each other. Tom stares at the floor.

Tom gets up and paces around the room, nervous.

GIRL. Ficky-fick.
TOM. Yeah. Ficky-fick. *(Tom looks out the door, anxious, waiting for someone.)*
GIRL. Ficky-fick!
KEV. Dear Tommy, How are you. I am fine.
TOM. *(Quietly.)* Leave me alone.
GIRL. *(Irritated.)* Ficky-fick, eh?
TOM. Yeah, ficky-fick! Five minutes! Would you just wait!? *(Girl, not intimidated, shakes her head dismissively.)*
KEV. I don't know why I did it, Tommy. At the time I wanted to chop off my hand and give it to the Tiger. It's a pretty intense process to remove your own hand.
TOM. *(Squeezes hands over his ears.)* Go away. Just get outta here.
GIRL. *(Arabic.)* B'ishreen dolar a-nam weya. *[For twenty dollars we can have sex.]*

بعشرين دولار انام وياك.

Ficky-fick! Ficky-fick!
TOM. I'm not talking to you! Shut up! *(Points to his watch.)* Five minutes!
KEV. First, you have to crack and break the bone. Bones, actually: There's a lot of them. On the proximal side: the scaphoid, lunate, triquetrum, and pisiform. On the distal side: trapezoid, capitate, and hamate. I couldn't fracture all of them. They're hard. And I only partially shredded my volar radiocarpal ligament. I worked at it, too. These things keep us together, you know? I never knew about this stuff before. But now I do. I am understanding how

things relate. *(Tom looks at his prosthetic hand. He looks at the girl, and then shifts away from both the girl and Kev, seemingly embarrassed of his hand.)* I'm just saying, Tommy, think about the physiology of the wrist! We are put together so well! And that Tiger tore off your hand in about two seconds! With just his mouth! How strong his jaws must be! How hungry he must have been! He just took it off and ate it. It's amazing how quickly you can lose a part of yourself. I am glad I met you because you are a true friend. Your friend, Kev.
TOM. *(Jumping up, shouting.)* I'M NOT YOUR FRIEND! LEAVE ME ALONE! *(The girl is startled. Kev exits, Musa enters, rushed. Musa looks sick, exhausted.)* What the fuck man?
MUSA. I'm so sorry … I'm …
TOM. Well, get the fuck in here! Okay. I'm sorry I shouted. Will you tell her I'm sorry I shouted?
MUSA. Who is this girl?
TOM. She's a girl.
MUSA. I can see that. Who is she?
TOM. I just need you to translate.
MUSA. You told me / this was for …
TOM. / Never mind what I told you. Will you just translate?
MUSA. Translate what?
TOM. Tell her I'm sorry I shouted.
MUSA. *(Arabic.)* Hoo-e mita'siff ala syaha. *[He is sorry he shouted.]*

هوة متاسف علا صياحة.

(Girl not impressed. Musa looks at Tom. Tom looks back at both of them.)
TOM. Okay. Can we take care of this?
MUSA. Take care of what? You told me we were conducting interviews.
TOM. Just translate.
MUSA. To her? I'm sorry, but I'm not that kind of translator.
TOM. What if I tell your RSO? I give you a directive, you follow it or they will kick your ass to the curb, Habib. Do your fucking job. *(To girl.)* Ficky-fick.
GIRL. Ficky-fick.
TOM. Yeah. *(To Musa.)* Ficky-fick?
MUSA. What are you talking about?
GIRL. Yeah. Ficky-fick.
TOM. So check it out. I been whacking off since I was eleven.

Always with the right hand. Probably at least twice a day since I was eleven, always with the right hand. That's a lot of whacking off. I didn't think about it. My name's Tom.
GIRL. Ficky-fick.
TOM. Yeah. Ficky-fick. It's not the same with the left hand. I broke in my right hand after all those years of yanking it every day. It had the right shape. It was familiar to me.
GIRL. Ficky-fick. Twenty dollar!
TOM. Tell her.
MUSA. Tell her what?
TOM. What I just said.
MUSA. *(To girl; Arabic.)* Rah yidfa'lich. Bess hoo-eh mistihee u-yreed yihchee shway-eh o-el. *[He will pay you. But he is shy and wants to talk a little bit first.]*

رح يدفعلج. بس هوة مستحي و يريد يحجي شويةاول.

TOM. Did you tell her?
MUSA. I did.
TOM. Does she understand?
MUSA. Probably not. *I* don't understand.
TOM. It's because of the shape! And the angle. I don't know! It's just different. And I can't get off. It's as simple as that.
MUSA. What exactly do you want me to tell her?
TOM. Tell her that!
MUSA. I did.
TOM. So?
MUSA. Even if what I told her made any sense, I'm not sure she understands what you want.
GIRL. *(Arabic.)* Inde floos weeyah? *[Does he have money with him?]*

عنده فلوس ويا؟

MUSA. *(Arabic.)* Inde floos oo rah yidfa'lich. *[He has money and he will pay you.]*

عنده فلوس و رح يدفعلج.

GIRL. *(Arabic.)* B'ishreen dolar a-nam weya. *[For twenty dollars we can have sex.]*

بعشرين دولار انام ويا.

MUSA. *(Arabic.)* Rah yidfa'lich ili treedee. *[He will give you what you want.]*

رح يدفعلج الي تريدي.

TOM. What are you guys babbling about?
MUSA. *(Arabic.)* Hoo-eh inde mushkilleh b'eedeh. *[He has a problem with his hand.]*

هوة عنده مشكلة بايدة.

GIRL. *(Arabic.)* Sh-sar bee? *[What happened to him?]*

شصار بي؟

TOM. *(Angry.)* You know that's very rude! I'm standing right here, and you guys are fucking talking on and on like that! Especially since I just kind of revealed some personal stuff and everything.
GIRL. *(Arabic.)* Shee-reed ysa-wee? *[What does he want to do?]*

شيريد يسوي؟

MUSA. She wants to know what you want.
TOM. What do I want?
MUSA. Yes.
TOM. I want her to stand behind me and whack me off with her right hand. *(Musa stares at Tom.)* Look, I don't care what you think about it, Habib, you're here to translate. Translate. Save your fucking judgments for your own time.
MUSA. I'm just trying to figure out how to say this in Arabic.
TOM. Fucking tell her and then get out so I can do my business.
(Musa slowly explains to the girl in Arabic, using gestures to aid his description.)
MUSA. Okay … Yireed-ich togfeen … This is crazy. *(Arabic.)* Yireed-ich togfeen war-ah u-tmid-deen eedich al-eh hette twen-is-ee. Hoo-eh yigool inoo hoo-eh may-igder ysa-wee heechee il-nefseh ba'ad lee-en foo-ked eedeh. *[He wants you to stand behind him and reach around and use your hand on him so he has pleasure. He says he cannot do this anymore because he has lost his hand.]*

يريد ج توكفين ورا و تمدين ايد ج عليه حتى تونسي. هوة يكول انو هوة ميكدر يسوي هيجي لنفسه بعد لان فقدايدة.

GIRL. *(Arabic.)* B'ishreen dolar a-nam weya. *[For twenty dollars we can have sex.]*

بعشرين دولار انام ويا.

MUSA. She will have sex with you for twenty dollars.

45

TOM. I don't want to have sex with her. I'll pay her more. I'll pay her thirty.
MUSA. *(Arabic.)* B-tlatheen dolar yireedich togfeen war-ah u-tmiddeen eedich oo testa'mileeheh al-eh. Hathe shee muhimm il-eh lee-en hooeh ma inde eed. *[For thirty dollars he wants you to stand behind him and reach around and use your hand on him. It is important to him because he has no hand.]*

بتلاثين دولار يريدج توكفين وراه و تمدين ايدج و تستعمليهة عليه. هاذة شي مهم اله لان هوة ما عنده ايد.

GIRL. *(Arabic.)* Sh-sar b'eedeh? *[What happened to his hand?]*

شصار بايدة؟

MUSA. She wants to know what happened to your hand.
TOM. I lost it.
MUSA. *(Arabic.)* Foo-ked-heh. *[He lost it.]*

فقدهة.

GIRL. *(Arabic.)* Shlone? *[How?]*

شلون؟

MUSA. Shlone? How?
TOM. In battle. In fucking battle, okay? I'm fighting in a war here and I got my hand blowed off and now I can't even jack off right. So tell her to get behind me and start me up. *Now.* Because I'm sick of this shit.
MUSA. *(Arabic.)* … harrub. *[… war.]*

فقد ايدة بالحرب.

GIRL. *(Arabic.)* Igder ashoof eedeh? *[Can I see his hand?]*

اكدر اشوف ايدة؟

MUSA. She wants to look at your hand. *(Tom looks at the girl.)*
TOM. Why.
MUSA. She wants to see it. *(Tom lifts and shows her his hand. She walks to him and looks at it.)*
TOM. Top of the line. *(The girl holds Tom's hand, tapping it, inspecting it. As she touches his hand, Tom looks at her. Something about her touch seems to affect him.)* It's not that hard. All she needs to do is stand behind me and then I can show her. I can help her do what she needs to do. It's easier than fucking. It's easier than ficky-fick.

GIRL. Hathee tilma'! *[This is shiny!]*

هاذي تلمع!

MUSA. Shinoo? *[What?]*

شنو؟

GIRL. Hathee tilma'! *[This is shiny!]*

هاذي تلمع!

TOM. What she say?

MUSA. *(Exasperated at the girl AND Tom.)* She says your hand is shiny.

TOM. *(To girl; loud, but not angry.)* Yeah, it's shiny!

MUSA. If you can show her what to do, why do you need me here? *(Beat.)* I am saying, you ask me to accompany you and that it is very important, but it seems you don't need me really all that much. *(Beat.)* This is a crude act. It doesn't need to be explained.

TOM. I *needed to explain it.*

MUSA. Do you have any aspirin?

TOM. What?

MUSA. I have headache. Do you have medicine?

TOM. No.

GIRL. Hathee mumkin tinshal? *[Can this be removed?]*

هاذي ممكن تنشال؟

MUSA. Shinoo? *[What?]*

شنو؟

GIRL. Yigder ytulle' eedeh? *[Can his hand come off?]*

يكدر يطلع ايدة؟

TOM. What?

MUSA. She wants to know if it can come off, your hand.

TOM. What are you talking about?

MUSA. She wants to know if you can *remove* the hand. If it is possible.

TOM. *(Suddenly angry.)* Why?! What difference does it make?!

MUSA. *(Also suddenly frustrated.)* I'm just translating!

TOM. Well, what the fuck!

MUSA. It's a simple question!

TOM. What, can I *take my hand off?*

MUSA. Yes! Simple question.
TOM. I mean, I *could*. But I'm not gonna. Look, would you just get out of here and let me … *(Tom looks over at the girl, who is for some reason sniffing his hand.)* Um, hello, excuse me. *(The girl laughs and goes to Musa, laughing.)*
GIRL. Reeh-et eedeh mithl il-haleeb. *[His hand smells like milk.]*

ريحة ايدة مثل الحليب.

(Musa laughs with her. As he laughs he sees something in the girl that changes him. He looks at her intently, but neither she nor Tom notices this.)
TOM. What? *(Beat; Musa watches the girl.)* What she say!
MUSA. She says your hand smells like milk. *(Tom smells his hand.)*
TOM. It does not.
MUSA. She says it does.
TOM. *(Yells at the girl, as if volume could translate.)* It doesn't smell like milk! *(The girl shrugs. Musa laughs to himself.)*
MUSA. *(To girl; Arabic.)* Entee shismich? *[What's your name?]*

انتي شاسمج؟

GIRL. *(Angry. Arabic.)* Shismee? Ente shismek? Laish ma-gool ismek il kul hel-nas? *[What's my name? What's YOUR name? Why don't I tell everyone what your name is around here?]*

شاسمي؟ انت شاسمك؟ ليش ما اكول اسمك ال كل هلناس؟

MUSA. Okay …
TOM. *What?* What are you talking about, it doesn't smell like milk.
MUSA. No, it's not that.
TOM. Then what?
MUSA. Nothing. I asked her what her name is.
TOM. Her name? I don't want to know her name, Habib.
MUSA. Okay, fine, she wouldn't tell me anyway.
TOM. What the fuck does it matter?
MUSA. *(Tired of this.)* It doesn't. It doesn't matter. She just … She reminds me of someone. She reminds me of someone I knew.
TOM. Yeah? Well, you remind me of TERP, so why don't you tell her what I want and then get the fuck outta here.
GIRL. Areed shwayeh muy. Gul-leh areed shwayeh muy. *[I want some water. Tell him I want some water.]*

اريد شوية مي. كله اريد شوية مي.

MUSA. She wants some water.
TOM. She ... Wait, what the fuck are we even doing here?
GIRL. Areed shwayeh muy. *[I want some water.]*

اريد شوية مي.

TOM. Fine! Fine, water! *(Tom goes to a bag and takes a canteen and gives it to her. She sits on the bed and drinks. Tom watches her and smells his hand. He goes to Musa and sticks out his hand.)* Smell this. Does this smell like milk?
MUSA. I'm not smelling your hand, Johnny.
TOM. *Milk.* My hand doesn't smell like *milk. (Tom walks to the girl. He offers her his fake hand to her, which she takes. With his good hand he tenderly touches her face.)* Ficky-fick. *(Beat.)* Ficky-fick with the hand. *(Musa sits and stares at the girl. The girl looks at Musa. The lights shift. Tom freezes as the girl becomes Hadia, Musa's sister. Musa doesn't see her, but senses her.)*
HADIA. Musa ... Musa ...
MUSA. Hadia ...
HADIA. Musa, when will you take me to your garden?
MUSA. You're not my sister.
HADIA. Musa ...
MUSA. You're not my sister.
HADIA. Of course I am ... of course I am your sister.
MUSA. You're not ... You're ... You're not my sister.
HADIA. I want to see your garden, Musa. When will you take me to see it?
MUSA. I won't. I won't take you to see it.
HADIA. But you've told me about it. All the beautiful animals. All the green. All that green you've told me about.
MUSA. It's not green anymore.
HADIA. Take me to see it.
MUSA. No.
HADIA. Why won't you take me?
MUSA. It's not a place for you to see.
HADIA. It sounds so beautiful.
MUSA. *(Filled with regret and sadness.)* Hadia, I'm so sorry ... I'm so ... *(Arabic.)* Hadia, ani mit'essif. Ani mit'essif. Hi soochi. Kulleh soochi. *[Hadia, I'm sorry. I'm sorry. It is my fault. Everything is my fault.]*

هادية، اني متاسف. اني متاسف. هاي صوجي. كله صوجي.

HADIA. Tell me about it.
MUSA. You've never seen anything like it.
HADIA. Why can't I see them? *(She touches his face and he looks at her for the first time.)* Musa, why can't I see the animals?
MUSA. Sometimes they run off.
HADIA. They're plants!
MUSA. Sometimes they fly off, to the moon
HADIA. *(Arabic.)* Ani da ahchee bjiddieh! *[Take me seriously!]*

اني دا احجي بجدية!

MUSA. I am taking you seriously.
HADIA. Can't I come and see? *(Arabic.)* Musa, egder ejee ashoof hadeektek il-hilweh, reja'en, egder ejee ashoofheh? *[Musa, may I come and see your beautiful garden? Please, may I come and see it?]*

موسة، اكدر اجي اشوف حديقتك الحلوة؟ رجاء، اكدر اجي اشوفهة؟

MUSA. Hadia … Hadia … *(Sadly, as if defeated.)* Yes. Yes. You may come to my garden … *(He lowers his head in shame.)* Hadia, ani mit'essif. Ani mit'essif. Hi soochi. Kul-leh soochi. *[Hadia, I'm sorry. I'm sorry. It is my fault. Everything is my fault.]*

هادية، اني متاسف. هاي صوجي. كلة صوجي.

(The lights suddenly shift back to the original scene. Tom faces upstage and the girl stands behind him, whacking him off. She has a bored look on her face. Musa snaps out of it, sees what's going on and quickly turns away. The girl continues. Tom yells out and hits the wall very hard three times. The girl stops and walks away from him with money in her hand. She exits. Tom leans against the wall. Kev enters.)
KEV. Dear Tommy, How are you. I am fine. I am glad that you finally got some pussy. Pussy rocks. It's too bad that to get off you have to have the chick stand beside you and yank it, but that is psychological. Don't worry. One of these days you'll figure out how to rub one off southpaw.
TOM. *(Yells.)* Go away!
KEV. Dear Tommy, How are you. I am fine.
TOM. I didn't kill you, okay? I didn't kill you. You offed yourself, and I didn't have any fucking thing to do with it. *(The garden of topiary emerges. The Tiger wanders through it.)*
KEV. It's not about whacking off, Tommy. You're not confronting the issue here.

TOM. Shut up.
KEV. You feel incomplete without your hand. You feel like you're never going to be *you* again. And so you think, "Oh, okay, I'll come back to Iraq and find my gold, and then I'll be able to whack off again." But things don't work out like that. Look at me: I thought I'd be in heaven by now, but I'm not. I don't know *where* I am. I'm just a reverberation of what I used to be.
TIGER. It's like God's revenge, you know? He's got us chasing our own tails here.
KEV. *(To Tiger.)* I don't got a tail. *(To Tom.)* Look, Tommy, I'm sorry I'm bothering you, but you're the only person who can hear me, besides the Tiger, and he just keeps bugging me about epistemology and original sin, which is annoying as fuck.
TIGER. At first, it's pretty cool: the limitless fruit of knowledge hanging low in your path. Then you realize it's the only thing to eat around here.
KEV. *(To Tom.)* I know I annoyed you when I was alive, too. But you were cool, not like those other guys. You were my patron saint around here, Tommy. Until you were a total prick and walked out on me at the hospital. I needed you, you know? But you were all like, "That's your psycho problem, Kev / not mine … "
TOM. / I didn't know you were gonna kill yourself! I'm sorry, okay? I'm sorry!
TIGER. What kind of twisted bastard creates a predator and then punishes him for preying?
TOM. I wish I hadn't done that! But it's over now. I'm fucked up with guilt, what do you want me to do about it?
TIGER. *(Examining a topiary shrub.)* I have to become something else. I renounce Tigerhood. I renounce myself.
KEV. We all have a psycho problem now, Tommy. Me and the Tiger and you. And I'm gonna figure it out.
TIGER. If this *is* God's garden. Maybe I need to become like these plants … twisting and distorting my natural shape into something more pleasing to him.
KEV. He's haunting me, and I'm haunting you … There's got to be some sort of relational algebraic equation that the three of us can factor into and solve our problem. I mean algebra was even *invented* here, you know? In Baghdad, by this dude, Abu Ja'far Muhammad ibn Musa al-Khwarizmi.
TOM. HOW DO YOU KNOW THIS!?

KEV. I know, right? I'm like a straight-up braniac in the afterlife.
TIGER. You know what really bugs me? Where are the FUCKING LEOS?
KEV. And "algebra" was derived from the Arabic *al-jebr*, which means "a reunion of broken parts."
TIGER. Why aren't they wandering around here, scared out of their stupid minds, contemplating their animal nature? How come it's me? How come I'm always alone every step of the way?
TOM. I'm not a bad person.
KEV. Neither was I.
TIGER. I'm a fucking saint. It feels like existence has become …
KEV. We're all just …
TIGER and KEV. … Refracted. *(Tiger and Kev look at each other.)*
KEV. *(To Tiger.)* Jinx. Sucka!
TIGER. Fuck off.
TOM. Kev, please, leave me alone.
KEV. We're broken, man. You, me, the Tiger. It's like we fell through a prism that night at the zoo and each part of ourselves just separated. Does your hand still tickle? Does it still itch? It's a phantom limb, Tommy. Just because it's gone doesn't mean it's not there.
TIGER. I'll become a plant, then. I'll cut away all the pieces of me that offend the cosmos. I'll escape my cruel nature. *(Uday enters, looking at the topiary. Hadia enters opposite Uday, looking around.)* But cruelty echoes all around me. Even in this ruined garden. And so, I wonder if there is any escape. *(Uday approaches Hadia, smiling. Taking her, lovingly, showing her around, showing her the topiary. He stops, sees something in the hedge … He takes out Musa's hand shears, large clipping blades for the topiary. He shows them to Hadia, who touches them, smiling.)* And I wonder if I am just an echo, repeating and repeating and repeating …
MUSA. Hadia … *(Uday puts his arm around her and leads her away, with the shears propped up on his shoulder. The lights shift back into the room with only Tom and Musa.)* She was too young for you.
TOM. What?
MUSA. The girl. She was too young for you.
TOM. What are you talking about? She was a prostitute.
MUSA. She was too young.
TOM. I gave her money.
MUSA. I'm telling you, she was too young.
TOM. It was a hand-job.

MUSA. Listen to me. Listen to me.
TOM. What?
MUSA. Listen to me.
TOM. *What?* I'm listening!
MUSA. She was … Too. Young.
TOM. Fine, she was too young. Arrest me. What the fuck are you still doing here? You like watching in on this shit?
MUSA. *You* told me to be here. *You* told me this was official military business. Official business! Ficky-fick! This is not what I signed up for.
TOM. Well, why don't you just leave then, Habib?
MUSA. *You lost your hand in battle?* I know about your hand, Johnny. *(Tom holds his hand, unconsciously self-conscious about it.)*
TOM. It got blown off.
MUSA. It got eaten.
TOM. How do you know that?
MUSA. Word gets around.
TOM. *How? (Musa gets his bag.)*
MUSA. I knew your friend.
TOM. What friend?
MUSA. The boy who lost his mind. He said you were like his brother. He told me all about you. *(Musa starts to leave.)*
TOM. Wait! Wait, Habib.
MUSA. What now?
TOM. You knew Kev?
MUSA. Yes.
TOM. Did you see … were you with him on that night raid?
MUSA. Yes.
TOM. Awright, look. This is … I don't know if you'd know anything, but Kev … He had a gold gun. It was gold-plated semi-automatic pistol. And he lost it.
MUSA. He had a gold gun.
TOM. Yeah, not that hard to remember, right?
MUSA. I remember a gold gun.
TOM. You do.
MUSA. Not easy to forget.
TOM. Do you have it?
MUSA. Do *I* have a gold gun?
TOM. Yeah. Do you? Because it's mine.
MUSA. The military is handing out gold guns now?
TOM. No, it was personal.

MUSA. It was your *personal* gold gun.
TOM. Yeah, it was.
MUSA. You must be very rich.
TOM. I was until I lost my gun. Do you have it?
MUSA. What if I did?
TOM. *What if you did?*
MUSA. Then what?
TOM. Do you have it or not?
MUSA. I do, in fact.
TOM. Well, Jesus, I mean … Let me have it!
MUSA. I'm sorry … *(Laughs.)* Why would I give *you* the gun?
TOM. Why would…? It's *MINE*! I'm not in the mood, okay? I got a headache and I'm stressed out so just give me my gun. It's mine. I'm serious.
MUSA. No, you're not serious.
TOM. I'm not? You want to test me?
MUSA. You don't know what is serious. You have no investment in this gun, it does not mean anything to you outside of the fact that it is gold. This gun has a history. But you, you're looting so you have something, something to take home. Well, I don't care about what you have to take home, Johnny.
TOM. What the fuck are you talking about?
MUSA. What the fuck? What the fuck are YOU talking about, Johnny?
TOM. My name's not Johnny!
MUSA. My name's not Habib.
TOM. What's your problem, man?
MUSA. You don't listen.
TOM. You WORK for us! I could have you fired, how would you like that?
MUSA. And what would you say, anyhow? That I stole your gold gun pilfered from the Hussein brothers' stash? No, no, there are rules for you. For me, there are not rules. No rules, nothing. Anarchy, yes. But rules? No. So go fuck yourself, Johnny. My English is getting better. Maybe I get a job at CNN.
TOM. You know what happens if they find a firearm on your person?
MUSA. How stupid do you think I am? That I'm going to just give it back? No. We will work out a deal. You get me some things, I give you the gold gun.
TOM. Jesus. What do you want?

MUSA. Do we have a deal?

TOM. What do you WANT? I'm not going to make a deal unless I know what you want.

MUSA. But you're willing to negotiate?

TOM. *(Enraged.)* I'm willing to kick your fucking head in, Habib! What the fuck do you want? *(Beat.)*

MUSA. I want weapons.

TOM. You want weapons.

MUSA. Guns, ammunition, and hand grenades. And then I will give you the gold gun.

TOM. Oh, yeah, okay. Because I'm an *arms dealer*, Habib. I'll get you a bunch of fucking weapons. Who do you think I am?

MUSA. You are a Marine and you are a thief.

TOM. Yeah, and I get you weapons. Then what? Next thing I know, you're blowing us all away? What am I, a jerk? You think I'm just going to give some guns and shit to a terrorist?

MUSA. I'm not a terrorist.

TOM. Yeah, then what are you?

MUSA. I'm a gardener.

TOM. Don't get metaphorical with me, prick. You're all the fucking same.

MUSA. No! No, you don't listen!

TOM. *What?*

MUSA. I'm a GARDENER! Do you understand? I'm not a terrorist! I'm not an arms dealer! I'm not a translator or "terp." I am a gardener!

TOM. Fine! So you're a gardener! So what?!

MUSA. You don't understand … / you don't understand …

TOM. / What don't I understand?

MUSA. I am an artist! I am an artist!

TOM. Yeah, okay, you're an artist. Gold gun. Where is it?

MUSA. And the weapons?

TOM. I'm not getting you a bunch of fucking weapons, okay?!

MUSA. Then you're not getting the gold gun! This is not complicated! Capitalism! Thank you! Now you want something for nothing?

TOM. What do you want with a bunch of weapons, anyway?

MUSA. What do you think I have to my name? A stupid job with the U.S. military? And what about when you all leave? What will I have then? I'll have guns and bullets I can sell because that is the only thing worth anything. Is that so crazy?

TOM. Yeah, it's crazy.
MUSA. I am tired, do you understand?! I am tired of making the same mistake OVER AND OVER AND OVER AGAIN. I always work for the wrong people. I always serve the tyrants. Not anymore. I am tired of being made a fool. *(Tom walks away from Musa, rubbing his eyes, exhausted.)* It's a simple deal. What you want and what I want. Isn't this how the world is supposed to work? *(A long beat between them.)*
TOM. *(Not looking at him; still rubbing his eyes.)* She wasn't that young.
MUSA. Do we have a deal?

Scene 9

A bombed-out building, half-standing, in the middle of the desert, south of Baghdad. The middle of the night. The place is ghostly, ethereal, haunted. Kev appears, as if he's been wandering in the desert.

Kev speaks in Arabic.

KEV. *(Arabic.)* Anee tayeh bil sahra'. *[I am lost in the desert.]*

اني تايه بالصحراء.

Ulleh, anee tayeh bil sahra' oo da ed'eelek, anee b'oomree me di'ait gebul, bess hisse da ed'eelek bgair lugeh. A'roof hathe shee ghereeb bess emelee inoo tigder tiftehimnee. *[God, I am lost in the desert, and I am calling out to You in prayer. Because I have never before prayed, I am praying to You in a different language because the very strangeness of it makes me feel like perhaps You would understand.]*

الله، اني تايه بالصحراء و دا ادعيلك. اني بعمري ما دعيت كبل، بس دادعيلك هسة بغير لغة، اعرف هاذة شي غريب بس املي انو تكدر تفتهمني.

Ukhuth eedee, ishfee gissmee ilmitgetta', ikhithnee min il-sahraa'. Khelee bal-ee yirtahh. *[Take my hand, heal my severed body, take me from the desert. Let my mind find peace.]*

اخذ ايدي، اشفي جسمي المكطع، اخذني من الصحراء. خلي بالي يرتاح.

(Beat.) Or not. Maybe, I should say a Hail Mary? I know how it works, Man: You're not gonna come down and explain everything to me. But I figure You're out there, somewhere. I never expected to know so much. I never knew there was so much to know. And the very fact that I'm *around*? The very fact that I'm learning all these things? I gotta figure there's something out there a little more important than just haunting Tommy. So what happens now, God? What happens now that I'm intelligent and aware and sensitive to the universe? *(Tiger appears.)*
TIGER. I'll tell you what happens: God leans down just close enough and whispers into your ear: *Go fuck yourself.* And then He's gone. *(The Tiger holds some small, indistinguishable bloody carcass, his face is covered in blood.)*
KEV. I thought you gave up killing animals.
TIGER. *What?* I was hungry. What's He gonna do? Punish me more? I dare Him. I dare Him to come down and tell me what a bad Tiger I am? Please do it. Look, I tried. For a good two to three hours I was a vegetarian. But guess what? Vegetables taste like shit. We're just stuck here, son. Mastodons in the tar pit of life-after-death. And I'm tired, and I'm not a saint, I'm just the biggest predatory cat in the entire fucking world. So I'm gonna kill something, and I'm gonna eat it and I'm gonna wave this bloody carcass in God's face and tell Him, *You knew I was a Tiger when You made Me, motherfucker.*
KEV. I wasn't talking to you.
TIGER. Ha. You were praying, huh? Well, you raise your voice and I'm the only one who hears it. What if *I'm* God. Did you ever think about that?
KEV. God ain't a Tiger.
TIGER. Maybe He is. Maybe I'm Him. Maybe Him's Me.
KEV. Prove it. *(The Tiger leans over as if to dispense a secret.)*
TIGER. Go fuck yourself. *(The Tiger exits. Kev waits for a beat for an answer.)*
KEV. Give me one sign to let me know that my voice is being heard by You? Then *I* can haunt *You* through prayer! I could haunt *YOU*, God! *(Beat.)* Your friend, Kev.

Scene 10

The same place: the bombed-out building, half-standing, in the middle of the desert, south of Baghdad. However, there is daylight, the place is less ghostly.

Musa and Tom enter.

MUSA. This is wrong. THIS IS WRONG!
TOM. Would you shut up!
MUSA. We need to leave!
TOM. I said we'd be fine.
MUSA. *Fine?* This is the middle of the desert! If the sun goes down, we won't find our way back to the road!
TOM. Would you relax? This is it.
MUSA. This is what? There's nothing here.
TOM. It got bombed.
MUSA. So where are the guns?
TOM. Just wait, okay? Just calm down.
MUSA. You brought me all the way out to the middle of nowhere? Where are the weapons?
TOM. Don't get pushy, Habib. Relax.
MUSA. No weapons? Then we have to leave. Right now. *(Tom gets in Musa's face.)*
TOM. We're not leaving until I say we leave. *(A strange woman in a tattered black shroud hobbles onto the stage. Her face cannot be seen. She has stumps for hands. Tom and Musa see her. They both step back and shudder, but Tom knows who she is. To the woman.)* El-salamu-aleikum.

السلام عليكم.

WOMAN. U-aleikum el-Salaam.

و عليكم السلام.

MUSA. What's happened to her?
TOM. She's a leper. There were a bunch of them living here. It was

a leper colony. Habib, ask her what happened. *(Musa looks at Tom, at the woman, back at the jeep. He sighs.)*
MUSA. *(Arabic.)* Hi sh-sar ihna? *[What happened here?]*

هاي شصار اهنا؟

WOMAN. *(Arabic.)* Kumbuleh. *[A bomb.]*

قنبلة.

MUSA. A bomb.
TOM. Yeah, we know that. Where are the others? Where are her … you know, her fellow lepers.
MUSA. *(Arabic.)* Weyn bukeeyet il-nas il-sakneen ihna? *[Where are the others who live here?]*

وين بقية الناس الساكنين اهنا؟

WOMAN. *(Arabic.)* Matou. *[They died.]*

ماتو.

MUSA. They died.
TOM. She's all alone?
MUSA. Yes.
TOM. Ask her where my bag is.
MUSA. Your bag?
TOM. Yeah. *(Musa starts to translate but then stops.)*
MUSA. *(To Tom.)* What type of bag?
TOM. What do you mean.
MUSA. You said bag.
TOM. Yeah, my bag! Ask her where it is.
MUSA. What kind! Big bag? Little bag? / Luggage?
TOM. / A bag! A fucking bag! Just fucking translate!
MUSA. There are different words for different bags!
TOM. Just TRANSLATE!
MUSA. *(Frustrated; Arabic.)* Hathe el-rijal yigool tirrek chees ihna, tu'ruffeen weyn cheesseh? *[This man says he left a bag here. Do you know where his bag is?]*

هاذة الرجال يكول ترك جيس، اهنا تعرفين وين جيسه؟

WOMAN. *(Arabic.)* Ya chees? *[A bag?]*

يا جيس؟

MUSA. What kind of bag?

TOM. I left a bag here, and I told them I was coming back and they told me they'd keep it and now I'm back and I'm not coming back again! Ask her where the fucking bag is Habib, or we're going to have a problem!
WOMAN. *(Arabic, calmly.)* Makoo ay chees. Makoo shee ihna. *[There is no bag. There is nothing here.]*

ماكو اي جيس. ماكو شي اهنا.

TOM. *(To Musa.)* What she say?
MUSA. She doesn't know a bag. The whole place has been destroyed. She's living in the rubble. She doesn't have anything. She doesn't have your bag.
WOMAN. Treed shwayeh muy? *[Do you want some water?]*

تريد شوية مي؟

TOM. What now?
MUSA. She wants to know if you want some water.
TOM. *(Losing his shit.)* I WANT MY FUCKING TOILET SEAT! *(The woman goes back into the ruin.)* What ... where's she ... where are you going?! Hey! *(Tom rushes to the ruin and peers in after her.)* What the fuck man, this is making me nuts, I swear to God ...
MUSA. We need to leave.
TOM. We can leave when I get my toilet seat.
MUSA. What toilet seat?! We came here for my weapons.
TOM. Habib, seriously? You really think I brought you out here to get weapons? I needed a terp. I need to get my toilet seat.
MUSA. So where are the weapons?
TOM. THERE ARE NO WEAPONS! WAKE UP!
MUSA. You lied to me ...
TOM. Hey, call her. Tell her to come back.
MUSA. You lied to me!
TOM. So what?
MUSA. We came out here toilet for a seat? Do you hear how you talk?! Listen! Toilet seat! Toilet Seat! You want something to shit on!
TOM. It's a *gold* toilet seat. *(Musa takes this information in.)*
MUSA. Gold toilet seat ... Gold toilet seat ...
TOM. Make sense now?
MUSA. I follow you around like a dog, everywhere. Ficky-fick, ficky-fick, the middle of the desert, so you can have sex, so you can get a toilet seat so you can shit all over this place.

TOM. It's a job, Habib. Do your job.
MUSA. *(Takes out the gold gun.)* Yes, Johnny … a job. A job.
TOM. Check it out man … my gun! You actually brought it with you. Holy shit.
MUSA. Yes, check me out.
TOM. Give it to me, Habib.
MUSA. You want the gun, Johnny?
TOM. Give me the fucking gun.
MUSA. *(Points it at Tom.)* You want the gun, but you lie to me. You want the gun, I want to leave.
TOM. DON'T YOU POINT THAT AT ME!
MUSA. *(Stops pointing.)* OR WHAT! WHAT WILL YOU DO NOW? WHAT ELSE CAN YOU DO TO ME NOW!?
TOM. I said we can leave when I get my — *(Musa shoots Tom in the stomach.)*
MUSA. Your toilet seat! You need a toilet seat! And you need your gold gun! And fuck you and your gold and your goddamn bullshit all the time!
TOM. YOU SHOT ME … You fucking shot me … *(Musa points the gun at Tom as if to shoot him again.)*
MUSA. *(His rage giving way to tears.)* I am tired! I am so tired of everyone …
TOM. Stop it … Stop it, please God, stop it … *(Musa stands over Tom and puts the gun to Tom's head.)*
MUSA. Don't pray to God. Don't you pray to any God, you piece of shit, man. No God is going to hear you. Not out here. Not anymore … no God is going to … no God is … *(Musa takes the gun away. He stares at Tom.)*
TOM. I'm sorry … I'm sorry … Please … *(Musa exits, quickly. Tom crawls and props himself up on a rock.)* Habib…! Habib, don't leave me here … I mean … I'm sorry … *(He coughs; he winces in pain. Long beat. The woman peers out from the ruins at Tom. He doesn't see her. She watches him. She calls out to him in Arabic.)*
WOMAN. *(Arabic.)* Treed muy? *[Do you want water?]*

تريد مي؟

TOM. Who's there? Who said that?
WOMAN. *(Arabic.)* Treed muy? *[Do you want water?]*

تريد مي؟

TOM. I'm hurt.
WOMAN. *(Arabic.)* Treed muy? *[Do you want water?]*

تريد مي؟

TOM. I don't know what you're saying. I don't understand. *(Kev enters from the ruins, carrying a duffel bag.)* Oh God, here we go …
KEV. El-salamu-aleikum.

السلام عليكم.

WOMAN. U-aleikum el-Salaam.

و عليكم السلام.

(Kev takes a gold toilet seat from the bag.)
KEV. Hey, Tommy. This yours?
TOM. Kev, can you help me? Can you go get help for me? I got shot, man!
WOMAN. *(Arabic.)* Yireed muy? *[Does he want water?]*

يريد مي؟

KEV. *(To Tom.)* She wants to know if you want some water.
TOM. Can you go get help?
KEV. From who?
TOM. ANYONE! ANYONE, okay?!
KEV. I can get you some water. How about that?
TOM. She has water?
KEV. I guess so.
TOM. Wait … You speak Arabic?
KEV. I kind of picked it up in death.
TOM. Well, how come she can see you too?
KEV. Dude, I don't know all the fucking rules / okay?
TOM. / Jesus. Yes! Yes, I want some water! *(The woman hobbles into the ruins.)*
KEV. What's it like getting shot?
TOM. It sucks.
KEV. Yeah.
TOM. Can't you go tell someone I'm here? Please, Kev, can't you do that?
KEV. Sorry, man. But this is the best I can do. *(The woman hobbles out from the ruins with a goatskin flask slung around her shoulders. She brings it to Tom and drops it in his lap.)*
TOM. Thank you. *(Tom drinks.)* Oh … man … Okay. I gotta get

back to the Jeep …
KEV. Habib took the Jeep.
TOM. Aw fuck! Okay, come on … What else … Look can you ask her if she knows anyone around here? I'm dying, Kev, can you ask her if she can help me?
KEV. *(Arabic.)* Sedeekee day-moot. Tigdereen itsa'dee? *[My friend is dying. Can you help him out?]*

صديقي دي موت. تكدرين تساعدي؟

WOMAN. Endee isa'fat aweliye. *[I have a first-aid kit.]*

عندي اسعافات اولية.

KEV. She said she has a first-aid kit.
TOM. She has first-aid?! She's a *leper*, she's got a first-aid kit?!
KEV. That's what she said.
TOM. Fuck, man! Tell her to go get it! *(Kev nods at the woman, she reenters the ruins.)* I'm not gonna die here … I'm not gonna die. I'm gonna fuckin' fight through this, you know?
KEV. At least you got your toilet seat.
TOM. *(Clutching toilet seat closer.)* FUCK YOU. *(The woman enters with a very old metal box. She gives it to Kev.)* Oh, God, thank you … thank you so much … thank you … *(Kev opens is, looks inside, dumps out the only thing inside: A single Band-Aid, which flutters down into Tom's lap. Directed at no one; half-laughing, half-crying:)* I GOT SHOT IN THE STOMACH, WHAT THE FUCK I NEED WITH A BAND-AID! *(He coughs, clutches his stomach. Realizes he's dying for sure.)* Oh, God … Kev, I'm gonna die.
KEV. Yeah, man. I know.
TOM. No … no no no … I can't believe I'm going to die. I can't believe I'm going to die *here*. Out here in the middle of nowhere. I'm from Michigan. It's shaped like a mitten. I was never supposed to die here. *(Beat.)* What happens when you die?
KEV. You know when you've been drinking all night? And you start to fade? And you can't keep your eyes open, even when you're talking? That's how it goes, man. It's not too bad.
TOM. I don't want to die.
KEV. I know.
TOM. Tell her … tell I don't want to die.
KEV. Hoo-eh mayreed ymoot. *[He doesn't want to die.]*

هوة ميريد يموت.

WOMAN. *(Arabic.)* Jissmi de-yit'akel ttul hayati. *[My body has been decaying for my whole life.]*

جسمي ديتاكل طول حياتي.

KEV. She said that she has been decaying her whole life.
WOMAN. *(Arabic.)* Ani masnoo'a min remmull. *[I am made of sand.]*

اني مصنوعة من رمل.

KEV. She says she is made of sand.
TOM. Can you ask her how long she's not had any hands? How long she's just had stumps. *(Kev thinks. He then asks the woman in Arabic.)*
KEV. *(Arabic.)* Yireed yu'roof shked sar-lich bidoon eedain. *[He would like to know how long you have not had your hands.]*

يريد يعرف شكد صارلج بدون ايدين.

WOMAN. *(Arabic.)* Min chan oumri arbata'ash seneh eedainatee wig'ow. Wig'ow shwaya, shwaya bmuroor il-ayam. *[When I was 14 years old they fell off. They slowly fell off over time.]*

من جان عمري ارباطعش سنة ايديناتي وكعو . وكعو شوية شوية بمرور الايام.

KEV. Since she was 14. She said they slowly just fell off. *(Tom shows her his prosthetic hand.)*
TOM. *(To woman.)* This is what you get now if you lose your hand. It's top of the line. It smells like milk. Don't leave me, Kev. *(The woman goes to him and sits by him and looks at the hand. The woman speaks to him plainly.)*
WOMAN. *(Arabic.)* Wala-shee. *[Nothing.]*

ولا شي.

Makoo Ulleh. *[There is no God.]*

ماكوا الله.

La jenna, wala je-hen-nem. *[No heaven, no hell.]*

لا جنتو لا جهنم.

Il-moat moo-shee. Il-moat musalim. *[Death is nothing. It is peaceful.]*

الموت مو شي. الموت مسالم.

Scene 11

The garden of topiary.

Musa enters.

MUSA. *(Hushed, whispered, to himself.)* My horse. My poor horse. *(Goes to another topiary.)* Look at you ... Such a pretty ... so lovely ...
(Uday enters.)
UDAY. Oh, Mansour! Uday is so PROUD! Stupid kid American. Ha! He suffered, Mansour. He died slowly in the desert all alone. And do you know what the best thing? He called out for you! Begging you to come back and save him! He *begged* you! Ha! Fuck me, man, you're good! That's advanced: getting a man to beg you to come back to him *after* you've shot him?! And shot him why? Because he was *annoying you*! Because he wouldn't shut up. I agree. Annoying people should all be shot and left to die. Because fuck them! Mansour. Oh, Mansour. Uday is so proud.
MUSA. You don't know anything. It wasn't supposed to happen. I didn't want to kill him.
UDAY. I know what you mean. Accidents like that are happening to Uday all the time.
MUSA. I'm not like you are ... I am not the kind of person who does this. It is not who I am.
UDAY. Sometimes we *change*. As people. This is the type of shit they teach you in boarding school. Like you: how one day you are translating, and another day you are shooting people because they annoy you.
MUSA. *That's not why I killed him!*
UDAY. *(Excited.)* Then why?
MUSA. Not because of that.
UDAY. You tell me. Tell me why. Uday wants to know. *Why?*
MUSA. Because ... we were in the desert ... and the sun was going down ... And ... *(Beat.)* The sun was going down.
UDAY. ... What?
MUSA. *(Quiet.)* The sun was going down.

UDAY. THE SUN WAS GOING DOWN! Holy shit, my man, that's your excuse?! The sun?! You know that happens *every day*, right? The sun *goes down*. Fuck me, even my FATHER needed better reasons than that! I thought you were good, Mansour, but this? *(Musa holds the gun out.)*
MUSA. Take it back.
UDAY. It's yours now. You've earned it.
MUSA. I'll never use it again.
UDAY. Come on! Not even once?
MUSA. Never.
UDAY. Don't tell me you didn't like it! It felt a little bit good, no? Killing the boy, leaving him to die. When you realized the bullet hit, that it caused pain, you felt *relief*. I know it, man. The pain *went away*.
MUSA. Yes, the pain went away.
UDAY. Good. You're beginning to learn about survival.
MUSA. It brought him to his knees.
UDAY. Yeah, yeah, and then?
MUSA. He screamed. He prayed to God.
UDAY. And you told him…?
MUSA. I told him not to pray to God. I told him no God would ever hear him.
UDAY. Nice. Good line.
MUSA. I stood above him and pressed the gun to his head.
UDAY. But you let him live. Better he can suffer.
MUSA. No. No more, no more … *(Musa gives the gun back to Uday.)*
UDAY. Mansour … you can't let go now! You have a taste for blood. You like it. You want it again and again and again. *(Uday holds out the gun. Musa spits on it.)* This is very rude, Mansour. Very rude. You know what your problem is Mansour?
MUSA. I don't have a problem.
UDAY. Your problem is this: The best thing you've ever done, in your entire life, was only possible because of me. Without Uday, you're just a petty gardener. With Uday, on another hand, you're the artist, building topiary, doing these great things. Because I wanted them. Because I employed you. Because I provided you with thousands of gallons of water in the middle of the fucking desert.
MUSA. This is my garden.

UDAY. No, Mister Fuck-Shit! This is Uday's garden! You think this place is *yours*? These animals are *yours*? Even your *memory*? It all belongs to Uday.
MUSA. No, no, I can remember a life without you ... I can remember my sister without you ...
UDAY. *(Beat; Uday leans in to Musa.)* When the blades of your shears touched her skin, she burst like a grape. Ruined my suit. *(Uday holds the gun out.)* Oh, Hadia. Hadia Hadia Hadia. Such a small creature, making such a great noise. *(Musa stares at him and then takes the gun.)* Good boy. You take it, and go out tomorrow, and find someone else. It will be easy. The sun will set and you'll have no choice but to kill somebody. *(Musa points the gun to his own head. Exasperated.)* No, Mansour ... Someone else.
MUSA. I won't be like you. I am myself. I am myself. *(Hadia enters, covering her eyes with her hands.)*
HADIA. Can I look yet? Can I look now, Musa?
MUSA. Not yet.
UDAY. Don't you bring her into this, Mansour! You do not want to see this again.
HADIA. I want to see it! Let me see the garden, Musa! Can I look?
UDAY. I will take her again, Mansour. I will do it all again. I will tear her to pieces again and again and again ... *(Musa leaves Uday and goes to her.)*
MUSA. You can look but then you have to go. But for now, Hadia ... Open your eyes.
HADIA. It's beautiful, Musa, it's lovely. Look, A lion! A camel ... an elephant ... a ... what is that?
MUSA. That is my giraffe.
HADIA. How do you do it?
MUSA. I don't know. It's difficult to explain.
HADIA. It's beautiful here.
MUSA. It is.
HADIA. Who could have ever thought, eh, Musa? That such a place could be here? That trees could grow like this? Who could have ever thought?
UDAY. Fine, okay ... *(Starts to move towards Hadia.)* This is not going to end well, boss.
MUSA. Hadia ... leave now. Go home. Go home quickly. Never come back. Leave.

HADIA. I'll leave in a moment. I want to see the rest. *(Uday takes Hadia by the arm, holding her firmly.)*
UDAY. You could stay in this garden forever, man. Watching me and her, me and her, me and her … Is this what you want to see? Okay, man. Watch. I'm going to take her back there and make her into a topiary. This time, I'm going to wear a bib. Oh, one more thing … That boy you killed … He was the boy who killed me. Thank you, Mansour. Thank you. Thank you. Thank you. *(Uday exits with Hadia.)*
MUSA. *(To Uday, but to himself.)* I will live with your voice, okay? I will live with it. It doesn't matter, because my hands belong to me. And my hands have their own memory. And when I put them on a plant, they create something. They will create something. *(The Tiger has entered and heard these last few lines.)*
TIGER. Look, I don't mean to interrupt, but I couldn't help overhearing … Did you make this place? *(Musa looks at the Tiger. Takes in the reality of a ghost of a Tiger before him, seems to be okay with it.)*
MUSA. I made this place.
TIGER. Are You who I think You are?
MUSA. I don't know who I am …
TIGER. Look, I've been looking for You, I've been calling out Your name.
MUSA. *(Covers his eyes in exhaustion.)* Too many ghosts. Ghosts everywhere.
TIGER. It's not just me. I brought this girl here. She'd been killed, you know? She was just a little girl. She wanted to know when You'd be back. She wanted to know how You made these things. All these animals. Horse, elephant, giraffe …
MUSA. This garden, this garden is a wound. I want to burn this place to the ground.
TIGER. Wait! I mean … The girl … She's not going to like that very much.
MUSA. *(Turns to Tiger.)* Tell her I'm sorry. Tell her I'm not who she thought I was. Tell her I've done horrible things, and I … I don't know what I'm going to do next. Tell her to forget about me. I've become a different man. *(Musa puts the gun in his pants.)*
TIGER. You're not a man. You're God.
MUSA. No, I am not. *(Musa starts to leave.)*
TIGER. Yes, You are! I've been waiting for You. I've been waiting for You to speak.

MUSA. God has spoken. This world. This is what He's said. *(watches Musa exit. He looks heavenward.)*
TIGER. *This?* This isn't enough! You have to say more than t[hat]. Explain yourself, for fuck's sake! You know what? You belong i[n a] cage. We should hunt You down and lock You up just like ever[y] other wild thing in the world. I can see it: God in a cage, righ[t] here. Finally get a look at You. And all the great mysteries of creation could be revealed at the zoo. Come see the God exhibit! Come watch the beast play! And we, the lousy dead, would finally have our Holy Land ... God in a cage in a garden in a burning city. Ohhh ... What a glorious sight! *(His eyes shut in a dream, a fantasy, for a moment. Then he opens them and realizes he is alone.)* I'm fuckin' hungry. *(He gets something to sit, and then sits down, staring ahead.)* So I'm just gonna sit back and wait for something to walk by so I can kill it and eat it. *(He waits, watches.)* Rules of the hunt: Don't fuckin' move. Don't make a sound. Be conscious of the wind: Where's it coming from. Be still. Watch. Listen.

End of Play

PROPERTY LIST

        ni-automatic pistol
        oilet seat

  y radio
  op
  ctionary
Combat gear
Prosthetic hand
Large piece of sharp metal
Severed head of Qusay Hussein
Cigar
Wristwatch
Canteen
Cash
Garden shears
Severed hand
Small bloody carcass
Goatskin flask of water
Old metal box with single Band-Aid

SOUND EFFECTS

Machine gun fire
Chaotic sounds: soldiers pounding on doors, yelling, screaming, furniture being overturned
Semi-automatic pistol shots
Bombs in distance
Muslim call to prayer
Jeep idling
Gunshot

NOTES
(ace to make notes for your production)